The Sparkle King
By
Patrick A. Roland

Patrick A. Roland

THE SPARKLE KING

First published in 2019
by Wallace Publishing, United Kingdom
www.wallacepublishing.co.uk

ISBN: 978-1-9996136-4-8

All Rights Reserved
Copyright © Patrick A. Roland, 2019

The right of Patrick A. Roland to be identified as the author of this work has been asserted in accordance with section 77 and 78 of the Copyright Designs and Patents Act 1988.

This book is sold under condition that it shall not, by way of trade or otherwise, be lent, re-sold, hired out or otherwise circulated in any form of binding or cover other than that in which it is published and without a similar condition including this condition being imposed on the subsequent purchaser.

This is a work of fiction. Names, characters, businesses, places, events and incidents are either the products of the author's imagination or used in a fictitious manner. Any resemblance to actual persons, living or dead, or actual events is purely coincidental.

Typesetting courtesy of KGHH Publishing, United Kingdom
www.kensingtongorepublishing.com

Cover design courtesy of
Greg Jorss
Upside Creative
www.upsidecreative.com.au

Also by Patrick A. Roland

Unpacked Sparkle
978-1944826314

Sparkle On!
978-1984514943

Patrick A. Roland

For Stephan and Chris.
You helped me walk when I could not and because of that kind of love, I can be anything, even The Sparkle King.

Contents

Prayer: I Had Dream 8
Prologue: Higher Love 10
End of Time 14
I Want to Know What Love Is 18
Coming Out of the Dark 22
I Still Haven't Found What I'm Looking For 30
Poker Face 36
Whatta Man 44
And I Am Telling You 48
I Will Always Love You 52
Water from the Moon 58
How it Feels to Fly 62
Bang, Bang 68
Ego 74
Faith 78
Bombastic Love 84
Against All Odds 88
Ambitions 92
Cherry Pie 96
Home 100
Dance With My Father 106
I Was Here 112
Hold Up the Light 116
There For Me 120
Moment of Truth 124
Waking Up in Vegas 130
Turning Tables 136
The Greatest Reward 140
Like a Prayer 144
Through it All 152
The Heart of the Matter 158

Epilogue – Life is Beautiful 162
About the Author... 166

The Sparkle King

Prayer: I Had a Dream

My dream is to be loved.
To love.
To be happy.
To spread happiness.
To be joyful.
To exude joy.
To show up for people I love and care about; especially to do so for myself.
To be a good son.
To make a difference to those who need it.
To change my life from good to great.
To always do the right thing, even when it isn't the easiest thing.
To grow.
To evolve.
To move through life with God on my side.
To stay in faith and recoil from fear.
To manifest miracles.
To create magic.
To choose God over and over again.
To be loved.
To love.

And I can do all of these things, as long as I continue to love myself.

The Sparkle King

Patrick A. Roland

Prologue: Higher Love

These pages are a bold and defining act of God's love for a wretch like me. It is my desire to stop hiding my true, higher self behind the facade of a character I became via "fame" and sudden popularity. Instead, I want to show you who I really am and all I can truly be, now that I have a loving and lasting relationship with God.

It is about admitting my faults and shining a flashlight on them, so that I can continue to grow into the man God wants me to be. It is about getting as real as I possibly can, so that I may strip away my ego and stand before you in all my bold and beautiful fearless vulnerability.

I am obviously not God, and that means I fail in life. Miserably. And often. But because I have truly found God, I also know true love. I know a real joy, one that comes from my deepest core and that is now in full display to the rest of the world. I'm not afraid to shout it out like I once was. I'm now up on Oprah's couch with Tom Cruise, only I'm not in love with Katie Holmes; I'm joyfully shouting about the power of God's infinite love and mercy from the top of my lungs. Because it is the God of my understanding who pulled me from the wreckage of my present and rocketed me into a new dimension, way beyond what I ever could have thought was possible for my future.

I have faced my darkness, and in doing so, I am claiming my greatest, brightest and most prolific light. I attract that which I am; and now that I know the power of my beautiful, resilient and blinding light, I can attract and reflect such light too. I can proudly promise you a life of the kind of love you always dreamed of but never thought possible. This is the promise of God, of living in the moment, of living in the power of now, and of calling Him in to your life and getting the BFF you deserve.

I am a beautiful, joyful, happy, loving, lovable, exciting, fun, amazing, awesome, resilient, glorious Child of God. And so are you. And this is the time to join together as a tribe of God's Light Warriors and fight the darkness, helping to bring others into the radiant light and love that I found as a result of continuously and consciously choosing faith over fear. The miracle of everything you ever wanted in life is on the other side of that fear. And even if you can't see the whole staircase, I hope you take the leaps of faith that I have. Because my God is a God of love and blessings, and as long as you shine your light and do the good work you are here to do, God will make sure you are kept in his protection and glory so that you get all the riches you deserve.

It doesn't matter where you come from or what you've done previously in your life. I am an overweight, gay, bipolar, drug addict, alcoholic, widow abuse survivor and I'm here to tell you that God made me that way and the God I serve doesn't make mistakes. You were born worthy because God made it so. You were loved by Him the minute you were pulled from your mother's womb; a precious gem and beloved child of God from the jump.

Your unique sparkle is needed to bring light into a world filled with too much darkness. And if you have spent far too much time, as I did, in that darkness, then all the better. It was all part of God's magnificent and marvelous plan for you. Sharing your experiences in that dark murky bubble of pain and despair are going to help someone find the type of joy they never thought possible. Yes, that pain you survived is now the rainbow in someone else's cloud–and God picked you to be just that.

We now shine so brightly, we could light the world up with the fire in our soul. Our pure desire could make the sun glow. Like every diamond before us, we have spent our time as a darkened lump of coal, forced to deal with the pressure of all the things life threw at us until we emerged brighter than a thousand starry nights. We are–now and forever–radiant orbs of the most dazzling light; precious gems of the highest caliber that are meant to shine brighter than ever before.

Now, because God made it so, if you make the decision to choose your light, you are in the midst of your own sparkle coming to life. This is when anything you set your mind to becomes possible. You are able to find the grace and gratitude in every situation because you know what it is to lack both. You are able to forgive your enemies and even pray for them, because you know what it means to be saved. You are able to sit in the stillness and let go of possessions and money, because you are truly able to listen to your intuition and follow the whisper that keeps pushing you toward the light. And if you are not there yet, that's OK too. Know that God will continue to shine His light on you until you are ready to bask in your own.

We were all meant to sparkle: the light is inside of all of us. God doesn't want us to play small or shrink back in fear in order to make others feel more comfortable. Instead, he wants us to stand tall, be proud of who we are, and move away from fear and into faith so that others like us can feel safe to do the same. God wants for us to be the love others need, to be the change that moves the needle on people's lives, and to be the sparkle that helps people become–like we did–who they really are.

Whether you call Him God, Jesus, Jehovah, Source, The Universe, Buddha, Allah, Higher Power or–fill in the blank with the name of your choice–He will be there for you and show up for you in a way no human could. More than any friend, any lover, or even your parents, who get old and become shells of the people they used to be because terminal illnesses have rendered them that way. If your best friend suddenly stops speaking to you with no explanation, or a person you want to date becomes abusive, or if a shady publicist steals thousands of dollars from you, or even if you lose your job and think you have nothing to look forward to, God will always be there. This is a love that never fails. One that is steadfast and dominant. The loneliest person in the world will know they are never alone with God on their side. Trust me, I used to be that person.

And so it is. God is everything or He is nothing. I hope you'll join me on this beautiful, brilliant and blinding yellow-brick journey of joy toward Him and His addictive love. Because this I know for sure: He IS everything; He IS the one and only Sparkle King. And because he made it so, I get to play one here on earth. Yes, even a wretch like me.

End of Time

On the New Year's Eve after my first book came out, I was carried into a New Year's Eve dance on a homemade throne.

Two muscled men pulled me by a rope into the center of the stage while four women–dubbed the Sparklettes–twirled and sashayed around me to the pulsating and joyous sounds of Beyoncé.

After a long procession, where I passed by the entire crowd of about three-hundred people, I emerged from my throne victorious: *The Sparkle King* was born! For two and a half minutes I gave the adoring crowd everything I had in me. Wearing a gold crown, a tutu, a decorated lame cape, and a sparkle-encrusted diaper that had all been handmade for me, I shook and I shimmied. I danced and danced and danced until the music stopped.

And then it seemed like I stopped too.

After what had been a series of consecutive highs and life achievements, I experienced what became a pretty major and ultimately scary period of depression, especially for an overweight, gay, bipolar, drug addict, alcoholic widow abuse survivor like me. The problem was, I was The Sparkle King. I had just written and released a book called *Unpacked Sparkle,* where I triumphantly declared myself sober, healthy and happy. I was walking around selling sparkle. I was all about puppies, unicorns and rainbows. But the truth is, on the inside, it was raining and I wanted to die. I just couldn't tell anyone because I was caught in my own story, a narrative I had written myself into when I decided to turn my pain into my power. I was afraid people wouldn't like me anymore if I was just Patrick again. I felt like I had to outdo myself again, but I didn't know how I could or even if I ever would. I felt like a grand failure even amid the greatest success of my entire life.

This deep depression went on for a solid four months. Now, I know depression; I've been solidly depressed since I was about nineteen. But when I got sober at forty, about a year and a half prior to this grand spectacle, I had realized a new level of freedom that had–I thought–truly made me happy, joyous and free.

But I wasn't. I was miserable. And worse, even as busy as I was with all the commitments I had with the 12-Step Program that had saved my life, and as popular as my newfound literary fame had made me, I was plagued with desperate loneliness that gnawed and ate away at me. This terrified me because I couldn't pin it on being a sudden widow like I could three years earlier, when my partner Pack had died unexpectedly.

I didn't know what to do. The problem with depression is that it's a liar–it tells you you're alone. It's a dark passenger that picks at and gnaws away at you, making you believe no one cares. It makes you think you can disappear and no one will notice.

So for a solid four months, I stayed in this abyss, not really knowing how to get out of it. I went full-blown hermit for a while–all the adulation and excitement around the book and the whole Sparkle King thing had kind of done me in. The truth is, no matter how long I am sober, I still don't always feel worthy of the miracles and blessings in my life. It was almost like I set myself up to fail, as I finally had everything I wanted but couldn't allow myself to be happy.

I want to say there were a lot of external factors that contributed to my depression–and people, places, and things certainly were not kind to me during this time– but the truth is, just like in every situation in my life, the common denominator was me. I was the one that was unhappy. I was the one who had to get out of it.

But how?

One thing that happened during this time was that I fell out with Bill, the man who had been my sponsor for the majority of my early sobriety and who had really laid the foundation for it. So I didn't really have a sponsor. I was still attending my weekly men's meeting and I had asked another man named Greg to be my sponsor, but we never really clicked, so that wasn't meant to be either.

Enter Daniel, a charismatic younger guy who was known for his blunt curmudgeon personality and brutal honesty. He was the complete opposite of me–but he had always stepped in and had given me great advice when my life in early sobriety was spiraling out of control. Even though he could almost be my son, the way Daniel carried himself–like he was the greatest thing on earth and that he truly didn't care if people liked him or not–was especially appealing to someone like me: a people pleaser who often feared others' opinions. He was also the director of one of the halfway houses where many of our peer group lived and congregated for meetings, so he carried a nonchalant cache that made us the perfect "power couple" in our sober group.

I was terrified that asking Daniel to be my sponsor would blow up in my face and cause our relationship to fall apart as mine had done with Bill. But somehow, I was more terrified of the noxious loneliness that ate away at me on a nightly basis. So, I manned up and called him. He agreed to see me the very next day. During that meeting, I would share my deepest secrets with him—things I had never even really admitted to myself—and I immediately experienced the level of freedom rendered when we get honest with another man and set our fears and resentments on fire by sharing and releasing them.

The Sparkle King was back, bitch! And because of that, I made myself believe I had conquered my fear of intimacy with other men, the kind that had eluded me since Pack's death. I spent the greater part of the next six months believing Daniel was my best friend and doing everything in my power to spend time with him and 'make him love me'. I even bought him a ring! Granted, it was just the kind of ring that the other men in our men's group wore, but I thought the act would cement *Dantrick* forever and that we would rule our Kingdom the way a real Sparkle King and his source of power should.

And it was amazing. Until Daniel called me one night and screamed at me for an hour about what a failure and a loser I was. He ripped into me, telling me my ego was out of control and that he couldn't stand by and watch me behave that way anymore. It crushed me. Decimated me. Destroyed me. My hero basically hated me. Also, my greatest fear was coming true: another important relationship with a man I thought I needed to survive was over. I was a widow yet again. This act of careless cruelty rendered me useless—and without a Higher Power.

Daniel was so mean and abusive in his delivery, it was easy to walk away. I had been a survivor of severe childhood bullying and almost deadly adult domestic violence, but I had set boundaries in sobriety. He was out of line. Everyone agreed. *Dantrick* was done.

But this time I was about to push through my fear and move toward the greatest miracle of my life: I would soon realize The Sparkle King was not me after all; it was God. I was about to stop making other men like Daniel my 'Higher Power', which was something I had done my whole life, and begin a powerful and life-changing relationship with the only one that ever mattered.

Patrick A. Roland

I Want to Know What Love Is

One of the greatest blessings of long-term sobriety is the opportunity to watch people grow into who they really are. It's a gift from God when they become your best friend and ease pain you didn't think would ever go away, just by showing up and being there.

I first met the man who is now my closest and most trusted friend when I'd had about a year and a half of sobriety. He did too, actually, but he was fresh out of jail and had not really experienced the miracle of service work in our program, so he didn't exude the confidence most of us attain as we grow into better versions of ourselves. He was a little shy actually; a man of few words at first. I'm often described as the loudest person in our group, so this was an odd pairing from the jump.

He was dating a girl who I had been friends with and even sponsored for a minute. And by 'sponsor', I mean she tricked me into paying her rent for her. I later found out she had done that to him too. We started talking because of her.

One of my very first service commitments was at an awful halfway house, where most of the residents were there because they were on parole and had to be, not because they wanted the solution we find through God and 12 Steps. The meeting was outside in the hot Arizona sun in the middle of our monsoon season, and if that doesn't sound miserable enough, getting through it was like watching paint dry. There are the types of meetings you lead where you can create fire and electricity in the crowd; where you see the lightbulb go off in people's heads as they realize what their life could be like if they were sober. And then there was this meeting. It was pure agony. It was me trying to talk over torrential rain and gusts of gloomy, dusty wind whilst ex-cons stared at their phone—or fell asleep.

At this point, I was way overbooked with service commitments and CP, as I now call him, wanted to be at that meeting because that girl was there. So in the art of pawning off this meeting I hated, I made a friend for life. I'm so glad God knows what He is doing because I probably wouldn't have given CP a second thought back in those days.

CP had a different attitude about that first meeting. This was his first commitment to the program. He took it and ran with it. Every time I saw him after that, he was grateful and enthusiastic about that meeting. It was a little overkill, if I'm being honest. I'm glad he liked it though, since I hadn't. I'm sure I thought I'd got one over on him at the time. It made me feel a little guilty, actually. Those feelings wouldn't last long though, as I was about to change his life.

As CP's interest in the program kept growing, I kept running into him. And every time he was kind, interested in what was going on in my life, and loving. So loving. CP is a jocular, always joyful and grateful man. Despite being a gym rat and a super-masculine jock who wears sports jerseys and wife-beaters, and who overuses the word 'bro' with no irony, he has no problem saying "I love you" and offering a hug that feels like the only one you've ever had in your whole life, every single time he parts ways with you. He is so present and open. CP is the dream friend for a person living with a mental illness, like I do. When he asks how I'm doing and I say "I'm depressed," he actually responds: "What can I do to help?" If I tell him I'm in pain, he says: "I'm sorry you are feeling that way." When I tell him I'm lonely, he says: "I hope you know I'm always here." Did I mention that he has never parted ways with me without saying he loves me? And yet, even though CP is just about as perfect as they come—and maybe perhaps because he is—I spent the majority of our early friendship ignoring him and chasing after

Daniel, who was often stoic and uninterested in me even though he was my sponsor. In fact, he was bitingly cruel and downright hateful sometimes—which made him more of a challenge, I guess.

Though I never gave CP the appreciation or true attention he deserved, he was always grateful toward me for giving him that first meeting that jolted him into a life of service. Apparently, it was across the street from where he had once often scored drugs. Going there every week not only gave him a renewed sense of purpose—it reminded him of how far he had come. He says it was where he had the spiritual experience that made him know he would never have a drug problem again.

Eventually, his service work ethic brought him to a committee meeting I was attending with Melissa, my best friend of more than twenty years. She must have seen us talking because she immediately wanted to know about my handsome friend with the distinguished grey hair that made him look older than he was—which would have made him the appropriate age for her. She asked me if he was single; I didn't think he was still dating that girl because she had moved away several months prior, but I didn't know for sure, so I told Melissa I would investigate.

I approached CP at our men's meeting and I think he thought I was asking him out because I started asking all these personal questions that were out of place at the time, since we were all business back then. I assured him all my questions weren't for me and asked how he felt about dating older women. He was in!

"What about much older?" I asked, tilting my head with matching bitch face and cackling loudly, as I often do when I am being catty. He was still in! So I set them up and they hit it off. Again, I had done a relatively minor thing that had brought him great joy. I was like his fairy Godmother, I guess. I even had the sparkly shoes and wand from my Sparkle King get-up!

Several months later, CP and I started doing a panel

meeting in a hospital together. Every week, I got the honor of seeing this once rather shy guy's eyes light up when he talks about how joyful and fulfilling his life is now that he is in service. I listen as his life moves from homeless drug-addled drudgery to a life of passion, love, and purpose, and I feel more loved than I ever have when he tells a group of addicts that he has all of it because I believed in him when no one else did.

I always thought he loved me so much because of the Melissa hook up, but it was actually because of that first meeting. The one that helped him grow into the man he really is. And though his kindness and integrity moves me to my core, I know it wasn't me—it was God working through me. And that makes both of us and our beautiful relationship—the closest I have experienced with another human being since my partner died—a miracle and a blessing. And because of CP and his wondrous friendship, which is like a mirror because the truth is everything I admire about him is actually true of myself as well, I no longer *want to know what love is*, like that old eighties song asks. I already know what it is, because he shows me every day, just by being my friend.

Coming Out of the Dark

Everything you have heard about me is true: I am an overweight, gay, middle-aged, bipolar, drug addict, alcoholic widow abuse survivor who is taking care of two elderly parents who are dying of heart-breaking terminal illnesses. I am also a joy-filled Child of God who is more unique and special than a million dollar bill. I can shake up the game and move the world with my God-given sparkle. And it is my intention to do just this until every blinding particle of the light I found in sobriety leaves my body and finds its way to someone in need of hope.

This light of mine – it burns so brightly. It would do nothing but give my fears power if I shrunk back and denied it. And I don't have time for that. I already spent most of my life—forty-plus years—as a victim. I now claim, own and inhabit my true higher self so that I can be the survivor, the brave warrior that other people need me to be.

All of the things that once destroyed me have now lit a fire inside me; one that I can't extinguish until I share it with every soul who needs the hope and inspiration I found within my life of turbulent despair. I lift my voice in power and strength, so that I may help those afraid to use their own due to stigma and fear. I believe God saved me from all these things that almost killed me so that I could do just this. This is my purpose—my calling—I am suiting up and showing up for anyone who needs me to help them find the glorious and life-saving self-love that I did. Yes, I love myself. And if I can, you can too.

The truth is that if you have a problem with any part of who I am today, then what you really have a problem with is God, because I know God made me in His image.

Furthermore, the God I serve does not make mistakes. If anything about me bothers you, reverse the judgement you have against me and take a good solid look at yourself. What bothers you about me is probably what you don't like about yourself. Take a look in the mirror and make the changes if you want to. Or don't. Just know that what you think about me is none of my business, so I won't give your thoughts any of my energy. Not today, Satan.

No one can take anything away from me now because I found my voice and my power, which many people know as my 'sparkle'. I'm here to say that what we do in the dark is what creates our brightest light. In my darkest hour, when I had reached rock bottom, I picked myself up off the ground and stopped living in a hopeless bubble of pain, despair and suicidal desperation. I am here to tell you that if you make the decisions to love yourself and to work a little bit toward your goals every day, you can find your own sparkle and live the life God planned for you too.

I wasn't always like this. In Kindergarten, I used to be afraid to go to school because the boys in my class waited for me every day with rocks at the bus stop. They carelessly threw them at me, spitting out venomous names about my weight and sexuality. Because I was five, I didn't even know what most of these names meant.

The fear and hopelessness this situation caused me never went away. This destructive and mean behavior shaped my identity and continued to do so all the way through school. Fear ruled me all the way through adulthood, too.

In third grade, my mom bought me a striped black and red jacket that looked just like the one Michael Jackson made popular in his *Thriller* video. I loved the jacket and was excited to show it off. However, I was taunted and teased with hate and hurtful words the day I triumphantly wore it to school. I was so embarrassed, I made my mom take it back to the pricey department store we had bought it at. I never wore a jacket like that again.

On the last day of sixth grade, the boys who either ignored me or called me names approached me with a present. It was a chocolate Ding Dong pastry. I didn't like chocolate, but since I wanted the boys to like me, I ate it anyway. I later found out it was a joke. It had been filled with laxatives, presumably to make the fat boy lose some weight.

In the summer between seventh and eighth grade, I lost nearly forty pounds. To go with my svelte new look, I asked my grandmother—a hairdresser—to give me a perm. My dad had always had one so I thought it was something men did. However, when I emerged on campus on the first day of eighth grade at a new school, the reactions were sinister and cruel. Now I was suddenly very gay—the weight loss exaggerated my feminine mannerisms—even though it would be several years before I realized that and boldly claimed it as my sexual identity.

Things got considerably worse in high school. I went to a fancy and pricey all-boys Catholic college preparatory school. I tried desperately to fit in, but my "friends" wanted nothing to do with me. At parties, they held me under water in the pool. Once, they tricked me in to climbing up onto a roof with them only to try and push me off of it. They called me a lot of names, but the one I remember most is 'The Whipping Boy'. I held on to that name for years. It seemed to always fit, no matter where I went or what I did to try and remove myself from it.

College also started rocky, but got better in time. I had decided to attend the alma mater of my mother in a small town in Iowa. I felt like it was my chance to start over and carve a new life out for myself, and I eventually did. But the first week started out just like everything else had. I was walking down the hallway and I was suddenly grabbed from behind by a crew of three masked men. They pulled me into my room, threw me on the floor and smothered and attacked me, beating my face with long socks that were filled with something that was supposed to make them look like giant penises. I think they were trying to mock me for being gay, but the fact that these men spent so much time stuffing socks to look like penises seemed gayer to me. Maybe something about me made them afraid of their own truth.

College was different. This time there were consequences. All of the men who attacked me were punished. Nothing like that ever happened there again. As a matter of fact, in my junior year—which was long before *Will & Grace* and *Ellen* hit our screens—I got honest in the back seat of a car on the way to a drag show in Des Moines.

"I think there might be more to this trip than just a drag show for me," I whispered to my friend Stacy, who was driving.

"We know," it seemed like she shouted. "Why do you think we arranged this outing?"

And just like that, on a cold, snowy January day in Iowa, I was gay. And though I now know I always was, because I was actually owning it, this newfound truth made me feel like I was the most of myself I had ever been.

Something magical happens when we break through fear and become who we really are. It's in this space that magic really begins to manifest. Suddenly, I was confident. I had no qualms about who I was, and for the first time in my life, people took notice. I was treated with nothing but love and respect when I came out. I even had some friends that looked out for me and made it known I was not to be messed with. Jason, a football player from a small town in Iowa who had never really encountered someone like me, was one such friend. I'll never forget how safe and loved he made me feel.

I'd like to say adulthood was better but it wasn't until I got sober, which was when I was forty. I spent all of my twenties and thirties chasing men, always to my detriment, and sometimes it was dangerous.

I didn't get into my first real relationship until I was thirty. He was a closet case in his forties who had never acted on his sexuality. He bought me a lot of gifts and played a nice provider role, but ultimately he never accepted who he was. It lasted less than a year and a half and ended one night when he screamed at me that I reminded him of everything he hated about himself. Those words stung, probably more so than any of the words all those boys had called me in school. They ignited a firestorm of drunken activity in me that soon became full-fledged alcoholism. I drank and drank to numb the pain caused by the loss of my first love, but all it really did was make me hate myself.

By my mid-thirties, I hated myself so much, I took up with a guy who upped the ante on name calling: he beat me regularly. He also kicked me and spit on me and trapped me behind furniture. One time, he threw me to the ground and chocked me to the point I couldn't breathe. Mostly, he screamed at me. He was a scary angry drunk man but the worst part about it is, I almost begged for it. In some sick, twisted way, I kind of enjoyed it. He was saying and doing all the things I felt I deserved anyway. I drank more and more to escape.

By the time that relationship was over, I was so ruined I decided to become a drug addict. I hated myself and wanted to die, and I figured drugs would finally end me. I put an ad online, looking for someone to teach me how to do drugs.

I met Pack from this and fell in love with him instantly. But he died because of drugs and I almost did too, due to the grief and addiction that almost swallowed me whole in the aftermath of his death that included being kicked out of my house and being forbidden to attend the funeral of the only man I ever loved by a very angry, homophobic family who wanted nothing to do with me because they were mad at him for lying to them about who he was for his entire life. I punished myself with a dangerous, almost lethal, drug addiction for a year and a half to get back at people who didn't even know I existed, until I tried to jump out a 26-story window in Las Vegas and end it all nearly four years ago.

***

I've been sober for nearly four years now. It is here that I have stepped into the power of who I really am. I now allow myself to sparkle. It is in this space of love and light that I've fallen in love with the man I really am. And that means I protect myself from pain. Yes, it still finds me. Life is life. Life is hard. Pain is an unavoidable byproduct of it. But it is not allowed to ruin me anymore.

Because I now stand firm in the power and strength of my sparkle, I get to work on pain the minute I feel it start to seep into my body. I used to let it hang out, take over and basically encompass me. Now I let it in just enough to feel it. That way I am reminded that I need to heal it, so that I can move on and keep growing in the direction of my dreams. Pain gets in; light comes out.

That doesn't mean it doesn't get overwhelming. For a few weeks at the end of last year, it seemed like everything was falling apart: a dishonest publicist stole money from me and almost ended my literary career. But the power of my dream and my desire to share the gift of my sparkle overruled his act of sabotage. It just made me work harder.

A man I thought I was getting into a relationship with turned out to be abusive. But this gave me the opportunity to show how much I'd grown, because I stopped the relationship from continuing. I don't tolerate abuse anymore.

A safe, comfortable corporate job became unbearable. But what really happened is just like in Vegas, when God hit me with the 2x4 to get sober; the discomfort forced me to push past my fear and leave a job I really didn't want to be in anymore.

The biggest whammy was the end of my relationship with a Daniel, my friend and sponsor. But there is even a rainbow in this darkest, most petulant cloud: I was able to choose a friend who really did want to be close to me. And if that wasn't enough, I found a new sponsor who pushed me to find God, which stopped me making other men my Higher Power. Now I have found eternal love through Him that sparkles more than anything.

Any one of the things I just described would have sent me on a life-ending drug and alcohol binge just less than four years ago, but all of these things now actually forced me to grow closer to God and trust in him more. This has formed a steadfast faith that recoils in the face of fear, as well as a new level of spirituality I never imagined. And because I survived it—and thrived in spite of it—I can tell you, all things are possible with God. You just have to lean in and face the sharp parts, pray for guidance, and be ready to step out of fear and into faith. And if you can't do that yet, just pray. Pray for the life you want; not for things particularly, but to grow into the person you are supposed to be. The person God wants you to be because He created you to be that person. Just ask Him to help you so that you can live the life you deserve. It's an easy prayer and He will listen: "God help me to become more of who I really am." Then get ready for the blessings, because God will always provide if you ask and then put in the work you need to. You gotta meet him halfway though.

I am ready for a life full of abundance and blessings. I am ready for all my dreams to come true. I am ready for success. I am ready for surprises. I am ready to manifest all that I have been praying for. I am ready to receive God's constant favor because I continuously choose faith over fear.

Pain pushes us to greater levels of ourselves than we ever imagined. So if you find yourself in pain, just wait for the power coming next. You're about to become unstoppable. You also must not forget: there's power in the struggle as well as great strength in vulnerability.

So, if you are worried about showing signs of either one, fear not: you are actually a rock star on the verge of leveling up to a whole new experience. You're about to learn who you really are, what you are capable of, and what you will become. It is when you choose to become fearlessly vulnerable in the way that I have, that you will find your sparkle—and probably God—too.

I Still Haven't Found What I'm Looking For

CP helped me wade through what I now refer to as *The Flood* in an unexpected way: by asking me to help him find a birthday present for Melissa. This was right after my relationship with Daniel came to an abrupt end, a publicist who promised to make me a star ran off with several thousand dollars, my best relationship prospect since Pack died turned out to be an abusive jerk that I had to kick out of my house, and I left my safe and comfortable corporate job with nothing more than a whisper to go on. That whisper told me that if I chose faith over fear, I would be rewarded by God.

Though I kept meeting up with CP to help him, what actually happened was he helped me, as he needed me in a time of great change, confusion and ultimate growth for me. It was as if God created that flood—a series of events to wash away what no longer served me so that I could move toward things that did—so that I could bask in the harvest of this growing friendship and everything else that began to flourish in my life because of it.

It was also around this time that I started seeing feathers—usually fluffy and white. My whisper told me they were a gift from heaven; a reminder that Pack was still looking out for me. They made me feel *Safe and Sound*, just like that song he always played for me. This was also the way I was beginning to feel around CP.

It should be noted that the first day we went shopping was on a particular Sunday morning. I found a clutch of such feathers on CP's doorstep. The trip would later become my alibi when that dickhead I was "dating" threw a fit because I chose to shop with a buddy over going to church with him. God was about to do for me again what I could not do for myself, and help me end this awful charade of a "relationship" that was now taking over my living room and ruining my domestic bliss.

CP had been dating Melissa for about six months at this point but he felt like I knew her better, so he wanted my expertise before buying her gifts. Even though our friendship has spanned more than twenty years, I am probably the last person Melissa would want to help buy her gifts. This is because I bought her a $20 Blockbuster gift card when she got married nearly twenty years ago. She still brings it up. I'll continue to pray for her to be more grateful.

The thing about CP is that he seems to know me and what I need before I do. So even though he probably did need my gift-buying prowess, he had most likely invited me so that he could be there for me in what had become the most uncertain point of my sobriety.

And I don't know if he was indecisive or if he just liked my company, but one shopping day became two, and then three, and so on. Then we had her birthday taken care of, but Christmas was around the corner, so we had to do it all over again.

The last time I was "unemployed"—I refused to call it that at the time because I knew God had a plan for me and I was just waiting for Him to show me what it was—I hated myself. In fact, I hated myself—and my mother, who had been distant and unkind to me when my partner Pack died—so much that I became a raging drug addict. This time, using never crossed my mind, but I will admit to the fact that having no direction is a bad idea for a bipolar guy like me. It's always a bad idea for me to have the opportunity to get in my head. These shopping trips gave me purpose and something to look forward to. It felt good to be needed.

CP and I had become much closer by this point. We didn't just make small talk about this committee or that committee; we talked about our lives and shared stories about our dreams and our pasts. He doesn't drive due to prior DUI convictions, so I always have to pick him up. And just like Pack, he always has a selection of songs that he plays for me. He shares their meaning sometimes too, just like Pack did. I even let him take over my stereo to play these songs, and I love these reminders of those long nights, years ago, that eventually bled into years of magical musical memories.

Before I knew it, CP and I were shopping two or three times a week. Sometimes we went to the movies or grabbed a meeting or dinner afterward. He even asked me to help him move out of the halfway house he had lived in for almost a year and a half, as he was going to manage one of his own. Another time, we jimmied a large couch into the back of my small Rav4. I had marveled at the fact that I made the math and angles work to get it in there—he brought out a manly side I didn't even know I had! The adventures kept growing.

Around that time, my new sponsor Reginald, the one who had replaced Daniel after he unceremoniously dumped me, invited me to go camping at an event where he was the featured speaker. I wasn't too excited about it. I was terrified actually. I didn't want to go; it was too far out of my comfort zone. But when I told CP about it, he really wanted to go. Even then, I was still kind of ambivalent about it.

As I drove to CP's house to pick him up for our adventure, I poured through every possible scenario in my head about what could happen in the woods. I would be bitten by a snake, attacked by a javelina, eaten by a bear, or worse—Beyoncé would surprise drop a new album and I would miss it. Suddenly, *Safe and Sound*, that Capital Cities song Pack repeatedly played for me in the months before he died, started playing for me like a lullaby. I instantly felt better. Then I got to CP's house and immediately found a single white feather—a symbol that this camping adventure was just another opportunity for me to choose faith over fear.

So I let go of my fear. Almost as soon as I had done so, the magic of that beautiful weekend started manifesting. CP and I got in the car and he started playing his music. He casually mentioned I was his best friend. That made me feel amazing, since the last person who called me his best friend was Pack himself. And even better things were about to ensue during that weekend. I told him that Pack's song had played like it always does, right when I needed to hear it most. I also told him about the feather.

CP is the only one I have let get this close to me since Pack died. I thought I had gotten there with Daniel, but he casually threw me away and punished me for doing so. Some men can't handle intimacy, I guess. And even though the demise of that relationship was the most painful thing I had experienced since the demise of Pack, God knew I needed to move on. As such, I knew this great new friendship was happening because of Him. I knew this because I had prayed to be loved again. Not in a romantic way, because I'm still not really interested in that, but in an *'I'm a human being and I need to be heard and understood'* kind of way. And CP is the most present friend I could possibly have asked for. He is always there for me.

As we drove to our latest adventure, CP shared his favorite road trip song, *I Still Haven't Found What I'm Looking For*, by U2. We sang along to it and a host of others. Rap and hardcore rock are mostly his staples. We got to the campsite and built our tent. We tried to take selfies in the dark of the night and this proved to be so troublesome that I laughed harder and more joyfully than I remember doing in the last several years. We just couldn't figure out the simple act of taking a selfie—which should be a cinch for a social media addict like me.

We survived the first night of camping. I got up to pee in the middle of the night and I was terrified when I heard something rustling in the bushes. I raced back to the tent because I knew that CP would keep me safe from whatever it was. It was colder than either one of us had prepared for. So cold that CP joked: "If it's this cold tomorrow night we are cuddling, because it's not gay if it's for survival." It made me feel good that he wasn't threatened by me or by sharing a tent with me.

The next day, we found ourselves on an impromptu road trip. CP needed cigarettes—and I was afraid we would run out of gas—so we went searching for both. We soon realized we were only about twenty minutes from a small town called Globe, known for antiques. So we went there.

Even though kindness is his staple, he still catches me off guard with how open and loving he is. For example, I had always called him CP because it matched his initials. It had become common to call various missions and adventures "Team CP," with the appropriate fist bump to accent our manly brotherhood. Then suddenly on that day, he said proudly:

"You're the P in CP."

"I am?" I asked incredulously.

"Of course you are. How did you not know that?"

I beamed from the inside out, feeling real love.

And then, for the first time in nearly four and a half years—which was how long it had been since I had found my lover on the ground—I fully exhaled. It was the only time since finding his dead body that I knew for certain everything was going to be okay. I wasn't ever going to be alone again. I was part of something, someone had included me in their very being.

The rest of the day was the single best day I had experienced since all of that pain and loss. I let go and just let myself relax and feel the stillness—the awareness of just being his friend. Something amazing happens when we are able to let go and let God in like that; I felt the presence of something bigger than either CP or I, and I knew for sure that there were magic and miracles. I also knew that if I kept showing up for myself and allowing love and light to enter my life, it would be there for me. Because I do deserve it and God wants me to have it.

As we traversed store after store, just as we had done

on all those now beautiful 'shopping for Melissa days' that cemented 'Team CP,' I knew I had found everything I was ever looking for: a true best friend who accepted me exactly as I was. He even proved this as he directed me while I drove.

"Go straight," he said.

"I don't think I ever can," I joked.

"I know and I wouldn't want you any other way," he replied, making me feel human and loved.

As the day went on and we relaxed into the jovial beauty and easiness of it, he turned to me and said: "It doesn't get any better than this."

"No, it doesn't," I agreed. "Any better and God would just be showing off."

Then I looked down and a beautiful single white feather appeared out of nowhere, as if to answer both of us.

Poker Face

Hurt people hurt people. So, if you ignore all the warnings—including the nagging whisper that the whole experience you are about to embark on with someone is a scam—and you go in to business with one of those hurt people, you're going to get hurt.

And boy, did I. To the tune of thousands of dollars that almost ended every dream I ever had about being successful in the literary world. But then I realized that what had happened was my fault. I ignored my gut and went into business with a known felon and liar because he inflated my ego and told me everything I wanted to hear.

About a year into my journey with *Unpacked Sparkle,* I made the mistake of buying into Sandy Bellows' grandiose promises of fame and fortune. At this point, I had achieved great local notoriety and success with my first book, but the national breakout I believed with my whole being was going to happen had still eluded me. I had a great working relationship with a publicist who resided in London, and while she hadn't landed me on *Good Morning America* or my hoped-for goal of *Watch What Happens Live! with Andy Cohen* on *Bravo,* she had produced a steady stream of online interviews and guest writing opportunities. Plus, she was always warm and loving—it was obvious from the beginning that my book was a passion project for her. In fact, she loved my book so much, she took it upon herself to seek influencers in the addiction and mental health worlds, where she believed my little book about grief, recovery and love would take off.

Enter Bellows. He had written a book like mine that explored mental illness and other similar issues. It had been relatively successful at one of the major publishing houses and he was even more successful on social media, where he had a massive Twitter following. My publicist had written to him to see if he would take me on as a client. He replied, saying that not only would he take it on, but he would also drop his rates and take my book on as a "passion project" because he "believed in it" so much.

I was leery, mostly because I was happy with her and not really looking to replace her; but she felt like Bellows was my best shot at mainstream success. She admitted she had taken this book she loved as far as she thought she could and wanted my success so much that she was even willing to pay some of Bellows' fee for me if I couldn't. I was humbled and moved by this grand gesture, but I wasn't about to let her do that.

I agreed to meet with Bellows on the phone, but what he didn't know is that I had also made sure Daniel was available and would be listening silently on the line for any B.S.

Bellows' performance on this phone call was Oscar-worthy. He played in to my hunger for approval and acceptance, promising to make me a star within less than a month! Not only could he get me on the cover of just about every magazine and big newspaper I could think of, but he could also get my book in the hands of everyone who mattered. A cursory Internet search proved he was who he said he was, but I was so blinded by the idea of all the flashing cameras taking my picture and my new seaside Italian villa that I failed to look closer and see that just under the Internet results proving who he was, there were a number of other ones going into detail about people he had scammed or celebrities he had beef with. Plus, there was the whole issue that he was a convicted felon who was jailed basically because he made up identities and then lied to people to get them to give him money. However, that's what the book was about and it all happened because he hadn't been diagnosed as mentally ill and now he had—and was supposedly healthy! He was meant to have changed; a successful literary star turned literary agent with deep connections and a posh Beverly Hills mailing address.

Though my ego loved his cavalier persuasion and casual yet urgent *now or never* attitude, my intuition had major issues with him. I didn't even really like him. He exacerbated my anxiety and seemed pompous and grandiose. Plus, it all sounded too good to be true—which now I know it was. However, when I asked Daniel what he thought, he said I should go for it.

"This guy seems legit," he said. "But don't come bitching to me if it doesn't work out." Daniel looked proud of me—his prize sponsee was about to be a big star—and so I went ahead with it out of a pure desire to "make him love me." That was my whole M.O. during that phase of my sobriety. It was a weird confusing space between early sobriety and finding the true emotional sobriety—and my relationship with God. Thus, I needed to stay sober.

And so I went ahead with an agreement I wasn't comfortable with: I would pay Bellows two large sums of money within a certain amount of time and he had three months to turn me into the next Eckhart Tolle. It was all to start on Sept. 11th—which should have been a warning of danger, since I kept seeing license plates that said 911 on them. Also, for some reason, his name always screamed at me in capital letters when I wrote it on my phone.

I kept asking: "What if this doesn't happen in three months?" And even though he never really answered the question, I still went ahead with our plans. When the ego wants something bad enough, it will destroy every bit of reasoning, even the voice of God that whispers from within, which was loudly telling me this guy was still a con artist despite his protestations of how medication and a proper diagnosis had changed him.

And so the scam began. I paid the first installment. I had to withdraw the money from my bank and then make a cashier's check addressed to him. Then I had to go to a different bank and send it to a specific account. It seemed odd that a reputable literary agent didn't take credit cards or checks or even PayPal—but I was about to be the biggest literary star since J.K. Rowling, so I didn't bother to question how bonkers crazy this whole set-up was. In retrospect, the whole thing screamed scam: there was no proof I ever paid him for what I was paying him for! He could say that the cashier's check was for just about anything.

Then he started his Jedi mind trickery on me. He was an amazing salesman ... just like any manipulative snake oil charmer of his caliber. He talked really fast and he was always going to or just leaving somewhere super-famous with super-famous people in tow. For example, one time he was "Just getting out of a meeting with so-and-so at CNN," which sounded super-impressive—I couldn't wait to be interviewed by the silver-haired fox Anderson Cooper himself! But I should have connected the dots: CNN is in Atlanta and I was talking to him in L.A. Nevertheless, he seemed to be making progress and he kept telling me how rich and famous I was about to become. He was good at providing lists of all the "yeses" he was generating for me—these were all from major newspapers and magazines. A feature in any one of them would have lit the match under my book and made me a star. The problem was, the list never changed. It was always "So-and-so said yes," and "This is a yes for sure." However, there was never an interview or photo shoot. He always needed "one more day" or "final approval." However, he talked so fast and enthusiastically that I just assumed that's how it worked in the land of Hollywood power players. Even though I had years of experience working for a newspaper and in public relations, so I should have known something was majorly amiss. For example, when I brought up getting my book to Oprah, he told me going after her was a waste of time and that it wouldn't do anything to move the needle on my success. But any average Joe walking down the street in Iowa—let alone a literary agent in Hollywood—knows she makes or breaks a book just by liking it or talking about it.

And then something that seemed legit finally came into my grasp. In addition to all the media publicity, he was also going to make me a star as a circuit speaker. There were thousands of dollars to be made in this line of work and he had all the connections from when he did it, so he would act as my agent and get me top-of-the-line speaking gigs at colleges and in the mental health industry—for an additional fee of course. He told me he could get me two or three thousand dollars per speaking gig, and again, even though my head knew it made no sense—I was far from a household name and I had no reason to believe I should be able to command such a fee—my ego allowed the charade to keep going.

I had forgotten that the second lump sum of money was due soon. The timing of the major coup about to befall me should have been a major red flag. However, he had gotten me two large-scale speaking gigs at two major colleges in San Francisco and he insisted that these were going to pay me more in two nights than I had ever made in a month of slaving away at the corporate job I hated. Then he sent me an itinerary that had me staying at five-star hotels that were so luxurious, I was sure to be rubbing elbows with Clooney, Mariah or Madonna. I actually wept when I saw pictures of these gorgeous hotels. Even the photography looked pricey. They were basically castles, and I was the Sparkle King, so it seemed written in the stars. I was ready to toss my imaginary beret in the air—I was finally an overnight sensation! On top of this amazing speaking tour of the Bay Area, there was another coup de grace: he had landed me a ten-minute slot on the most popular show on NPR the day before I was due to leave.

Eight to ten million people were going to hear my story and then I was going to board a plane the next day and be the next big overnight Californian sensation. He even sent fake questions for me to answer beforehand, so I would be ready for my big public unveiling. Oh, and by the way, the rest of the money was due, like, right now.

So I again complied, even though none of my questions had been answered, the biggest of which was "When am I leaving?" I was due to speak on Friday night and it was Wednesday, yet he still had not provided me with a plane ticket because the universities were apparently haggling over who was paying.

Then, on Wednesday night, after I had sent a series of increasingly anxious texts and phone calls about my flight in less than thirty-six hours, he pulled the rug out from under me: the trip was cancelled. One of the universities had pulled out and he didn't think it made any sense for me to go and speak just once. Even though I told him I was happy to do it, as it was an excellent opportunity for an aspiring yet-to-be-known author like me, my *California Dreaming Book Tour 2017* was officially dead.

"Let's get in touch tomorrow after your NPR interview to re-strategize," he cooed.

But that turned out to be fake news too. I woke up and was prepared to take the phone call at the time he had promised they would call, but that time came and my phone never rang. Nor did it ten minutes later, twenty minutes later, or at any time that day. He had not even given me a contact to call at NPR to check in with, which is public relations 101, but I didn't need one to know that I had been played. The jig was up and I had been totally bamboozled. He really deserved an award for his whole performance. It was seamless.

By this point, Daniel and I had already had our falling out. Also, I had quit my job the week before thinking I was about to become the next big circuit speaker, and the man I thought I was going to marry had shown his true colors and was gone because I had kicked him out when he insulted my dead lover.

I was in a world of hurt. But I never blamed anyone

for any of it, unlike when I was addicted. It also never dawned on me to use. No, my ego and blinding desire to succeed in all the wrong ways had caused this. The only way out of it was to forgive all parties, accept responsibility for my part in it, walk away, and move on. There would be no begging, no revenge, no wallowing in all the misery that had befallen me—all the staples of my past. I ceased fighting; I decided to forgive Bellows and assume responsibility for my part in this. After all, I was a willing participant in the whole charade. I even *knew* it was a charade! It had all happened because I ignored all the signals and all the signs—even the flashing neon ones. It was all my fault, no one else's. I never talked to him again, but I have prayed for him like I do anyone who hurts me. Like I said before, hurt people hurt people. I should have known better. It makes me sad that he has to get one over on people to make a living. I pray he finds peace.

And again, because of all of this, I found amazing power in a blitzkrieg of pain. The next thing I did, surprised me—and changed my life forever. I followed the suggestion of my new sponsor, Reginald: I got on my hands and knees and started praying. And that's when I stopped chasing all the wrong men and began developing a relationship with the only right one.

The Sparkle King

Whatta Man

Daniel was an asshole. I'm not being out of line or judgmental in saying so. He would even cop to it. He got off on it, being above everyone and making sure everyone knew it.

Being in the presence of a man with so much power and overblown self-esteem was intoxicating. It was almost like the less he cared, the more I did. It was a game to him and he always won, until you got too close and figured out it was all just a façade, not unlike the scary, blustery Wizard of Oz who was really a cowardly man hiding behind a flashy exterior. And yes, I'm fine being Dorothy in this metaphor. I even have the right shoes. I wasn't fine, however, with being sent back to Kansas on his broom.

Daniel was always a known entity in my sobriety because he was the sponsee of the first guy who befriended me in our 12 Step Program. His sponsor, Carter, a goofy guy who loved music and who was always looking for something fun and out of the box to do, was my closest friend through most of my early sobriety. We went on trips out of town together, hit up various sober conventions and when my first book came out, it was he who started calling me The Sparkle King.

Right around the time I'd had a year sobriety, I began an ill-advised courtship with a newcomer. His sponsor happened to be Daniel, who I knew but didn't really interact with yet. However, I was about to: he was directing a fundraising murder mystery play and I was to be his star. Daniel is the type of person who rolls his eyes and seems annoyed by just about everything, so my boyfriend loved getting him worked up and often regaled me with tales of bad behavior that exasperated

The Sparkle King

Daniel.

When I earned my year of sobriety, I planned a dinner party to coincide with my new boyfriend's thirtieth birthday. I didn't invite him, but Daniel actually showed up at it.

The next day was the first day of rehearsals for our play. I was scrolling through Facebook when I saw pictures of my boyfriend—the one I had feted with a glorious party the night before—naked in a hot tub with another man. It was the most disgusting, hurtful and surprising thing I had experienced whilst sober. The sheer pain of it caused me to shake with intensity and feel physically ill. I went red. Obviously, I wanted to know why my man was naked in a hot tub with another man. Even more, I wanted to know why it was on Facebook. The whole thing was so absurd, I felt it had to be a joke.

But it wasn't. When I confronted my boyfriend all I got was excuses, attitude, and blame for causing it to happen in the first place by being too nice. He was adamant the whole thing wasn't sexual, that I was over-reacting, and that he wasn't sorry.

It was not hard to immediately dump him, which was not normal behavior for a raging codependent like me. I had stayed with one boyfriend for years longer than anyone thought I should, despite the fact he beat me on a regular basis. I thought that was what I deserved—and loved being able to get away with lying about it. Then I became a raging drug addict to satiate the next one—the good one—my beautiful, now long-gone Pack.

This felt different. The sheer level of obnoxiousness was off the charts. It was a literal slap in the face. The truth was, I wasn't as bothered by the possible cheating as I was by the blasé way it was plastered on Facebook for everyone to see. It was grossly disrespectful, beyond hurtful, and completely unforgivable behavior. I had a reputation to uphold and the naked dude in the hot tub was not about to steal my sparkle.

It was over.

But all of this was happening in the middle of the first rehearsal for our play, and as I shared screenshots and *"Oh my God, how could he's"* with all of my nearest and dearest, Daniel had a show to put on and wasn't having any of my earned drama. He took my phone away from me and wouldn't give it back until rehearsal was over. I kind of loved the power Daniel already had over me and the charismatic 'I don't give a fuck' way in which he did things.

Being in that play at that particular time in my life was probably God doing for me what I couldn't do for myself, because it kept me busy. This was the first relationship I had been in since Pack had died. Nobody knew this, but until something stopped me—perhaps a whisper from God that the timing wasn't right—I had planned on asking him to marry me at that party. Little did I know, he would cheat on me the very next day.

Despite being busy, I was hurt, and I was 'acting out' a bit. This acting out and attention-seeking would become a staple of my odd, codependent, way-too-attached relationship with Daniel, who seemed to enjoy my flamboyant flair and excessive whimsy. I think he admired my over-the-top gayness and the spectacle of me joyfully sashaying around every room I was in—not that he would ever admit it.

Nevertheless, I was distracted and being really messy about it all. As such, Daniel pulled me aside. Never one for a lot of words, he looked at me and said: "What exactly did you expect anyway?"

"What do you mean?" I asked, half surprised by the question and kind of excited he was taking an interest in me.

"Why would someone with as much as you have to offer, date someone like that anyway?" His kindness moved—and shocked—me. I didn't even think I really existed to him. It was the straight man's equivalent of dropping the mic and it gave me the power I needed to dump the loser and never look back. I had never been able to do something like that before—dump someone who didn't treat me right. But this time I did. So whether he knew it or not, Daniel had helped me get through one of the most difficult times in my sobriety. He had also made an impact on me personally. I saw through his rough, I'm-never-going-to-let-anyone-see-I-am-really-human exterior and felt like we had connected on a real friendship level.

For the next several months, we shared a cordial friendship but nothing as close as that moment ever happened again. He chaired a New Year's Eve committee that I was on. This was the very group that decided I was to be *The Sparkle King* and since he was chair of the event, this meant his seal of approval was on it. I desperately wanted him to like me, which meant I had to make this whole thing work, even though it seemed so much bigger than I actually thought I was.

And so, under Daniel's watch on New Year's Eve, about six weeks after my book came out—it should be noted, he came to my book release party and seemed the proudest person there—I became The Sparkle King. Looking back though, Daniel ignored me for most of that night, even when I danced for our fellowship in a glittery costume. It was actually Reginald who stood behind me on the stage during the whole spectacle, asking the crowd to cheer for me and dance with me. However, just like in the early days of my relationship with CP, I couldn't see that; I was too busy trying to get Daniel's attention.

I had no idea how much of an impact Daniel would have on the next year of my life. First as my new sponsor and then as my "best friend." Then, as a sudden enemy, who chased me away for seemingly no reason, forcing me to find a new sponsor, and ultimately the real and only Sparkle King: God.

Patrick A. Roland

And I am Telling You

It's been almost six months since Daniel phoned and dropped the atomic bomb that then decimated me with his caustic and casual cruelness.

I still don't know what I did to him or why he still won't speak to me. The rest of my life is the one I want now, but the sudden departure of the first man I became close to after several years of intense grief still leaves a gaping hole in my heart. On one hand, he was so beyond hurtful that night on the phone that I'm glad I don't have to deal with his dramatic mood swings anymore. On the other, it's hard to stop loving someone who helped you find yourself and who was such a formidable influence in your life.

But if I know anything about heartbreak, I know the best way to move through it is to go through it. Like all pain, you have to feel it to heal it. The things that break you actually end up making you when you lean into them and stop giving them power over you. When you accept it, you take back your power and grow through what you go through.

I didn't know how to outdo myself after the whole Sparkle King spectacle. If I'm being honest, the crowd might have seemed confused if not completely disinterested in the whole thing, and that made me feel weird. None of it was my idea—it had been cooked up by a whole committee of people! I guess being a published author carried some kind of cache in a world of drug addicts, as they don't usually do things like that. Thus, they admired me for it. But having self-esteem was never my forte, and I had also never achieved so much notoriety, so the subsequent "fall from grace" with the shitty committee in my head seemed obvious to me, in retrospect.

I spent nearly four months afterward in hiding. While I fell apart inwardly, on the outside I exhibited almost diva-like behavior that caused my ego to rage uncontrollably and take out just about everyone who mattered. Especially my first sponsor, Bill. He had been the one who had made my sudden popularity possible in the first place by introducing me to everyone he knew when I was new.

Things got so bad, I found myself sitting across from my grief counselor yet again. Cissy Houston—I call her this since she looks and, I imagine, acts like my dear Whitney Houston's mother—was there for me yet again, only this time I didn't feel like my pain was connected with Pack. I was really healthy about his death and I had made peace with it.

Still, I was lonely. So lonely. It literally felt like there was a hole in my heart. I know now that this hole was so big because I wasn't filling it with the only person who really can: God.

Cissy and I agreed that I needed to get a new sponsor immediately. I had one but if I'm being honest, the reason I picked him was that he and Bill were enemies and I thought it would hurt Bill if I picked someone he didn't like. I even asked my friends Mary and June—who I had dubbed my Sparklewhores because they wore home-made sparkly t-shirts with that written on it to my book launch party—who they thought would hurt Bill the most. We all picked Greg. And when you pick a sponsor for a shady, no-good reason like that, it shouldn't be a surprise when it doesn't work out. I just couldn't—and maybe wouldn't—get close to him. I felt betrayed by Bill—though the truth is, I betrayed him with my caustic and exceptionally wicked tongue, insulting and hurting him instead of telling him how much pain I was in or how much he really meant to me. The other truth is I actually really admire Greg, and he was a great sponsor and he is an even better person. I just wouldn't let him be any of those things to me because I was being vindictive and immature.

Remembering that day when Daniel had pulled me aside and made me realize my worth after my break-up, I had been wanting to ask him to be my sponsor. But I was also kind of afraid of him. Also, I was especially fearful—the whisper again?—that if he was my sponsor it would ruin any possible friendship.

But since I felt like he had seen the 'real me,' Daniel was really the only choice. So I called him. He agreed to see me the next day. I thought I'd found a new kind of freedom in the relationship and the work we did together when we re-did my steps after a year and a half of sobriety.

But the truth is, that was all a lie. I was actually in Daniel's shadow the whole time. Furthermore, I put myself there because it was easier and safer for me than putting myself out there like I had done before, when I released a tell-all memoir about all the darkest things I had ever done. Those things that, for the record, I had decided ultimately made me beautiful. It was safer than being pushed through a crowd on a throne and dancing in front of them in a sparkle-encrusted tutu. And it was far safer than forming the real relationship with God I needed in order to move into emotional sobriety. Ironically, while everyone around me called me The Sparkle King, I shined less than I ever had since I had gotten sober.

I was actually in another desperate codependent relationship, only this time I felt like I had to outdo myself to make Daniel love me. I lost myself and my new inspiring voice in this toxic and intoxicating pairing. On the outside, it seemed like I was more popular than ever because of my association with Daniel. However, in reality, I was like the big girl in *Dreamgirls*. I was constantly auditioning to be Daniel's star—like when I had been in that play; or when he pulled me aside and told me what anyone could see, that I deserved better than a sucked-up newcomer who couldn't stay sober; or when I danced for everyone as The Sparkle King. I was so far from my true self that I believe God caused a flood so he could wipe away what no longer served me. He prepared me for the harvest of love, inner peace and intense personal power I found as a result of yet more pain I didn't think I could handle.

I Will Always Love You

For the better part of six months, I allowed myself to be another man's bitch. I even liked it.

It did not seem like that at the time. I was so busy trying to be one half of the program's most lucrative power couple, I didn't even care that I was about to stop all my dreams from manifesting, or that I walked around with a blazing ego, or that I bought a grown man a Diet Coke every time I saw him, just to make him happy. And for the record, I saw him nearly every single day, because I was a co-dependent mess who made myself so available.

As oblivious as I was to my self-destructive behavior during this time frame, I can say that I was prolific. I was in just about every committee in our fellowship, and because Daniel was usually the chair, that meant I was almost always the co-chair.

I remember standing in front of hundreds of loving people that I loved too. It was at a huge event and I was spouting a message of hope and independence while only caring if Daniel could see his protégée shining. I remember doing that a lot actually. His opinion was the only one that mattered. And when I didn't get the praise or love I thought I needed from him, it felt like I was suffocating and even dying.

If Daniel snapped his fingers, I came running. I studied him so much and made myself so available that I began to predict what he wanted before he even asked for it. Hence an unlimited stream of Diet Coke cans and yes, eventually a ring—which he had asked for, by the way.

As I'm writing this, the whole relationship seems so absurd that I can't believe I really was *that guy*. But I was. And it was sad and pathetic. And it went on and on for several months. Months and months where I ignored real friends like CP and his girlfriend—my best friend—Melissa, to chase around a straight guy and earn his approval and love. This was all because I was still a broken little gay boy who felt his father had never loved him enough.

It should be noted that Daniel was actually a generic archetype for me—he certainly wasn't the first man I chased around like this. However, because I have identified the problem—I needed God—and I've done the work on myself to find and nurture the real relationship with God that I needed to make myself whole, he will be the last.

Still, when that phone call came, I was never more surprised that the bottom had suddenly fallen out of this relationship. Especially as he had become the very reason I was existing. He dismissed me and everything about me like a tsunami. I had not experienced brutality like this since I met my dead closeted lover's family and was instantly forbidden to be in my home and at his funeral. His behavior actually hurt more because I thought he was my best friend.

Just before, I thought I had impressed everyone by trying to play football with all the guys. I had always felt a lot of personal pain about not being an athlete, so I thought showing up uninvited for a Saturday morning practice—and completely sucking at it—would cement my place in the group. It actually did with everyone, except the only person who really mattered—Daniel. He was wearing a ring I'd had made for him at the time, because he had told me to get it for him. By this point, Daniel was also inviting me to the movies on an almost weekly basis. The very last time we hung out, we had even enjoyed a really nice meal at a relatively pricey restaurant.

I remember going home from that dinner/movie combo and thinking I was happier than I ever had been and hoping my life was always going to be like that. I lay on my new couch thinking I was the luckiest person in the world. I might have even cried. The couch I was lying on was the same one Daniel had made me get when he had redecorated my living room. He had even made me a handmade dog pen from scratch because he couldn't believe I lived in such squalor. I thought this was so kind at the time, even though he charged me $15 an hour for all the work he did.

I'm so relieved to know that God always knows better.

At about 9 p.m. on a Wednesday night, the phone rang. It was Daniel. It wasn't odd for him to call because we were on about fourteen committees together and he was my sponsor, but the tone in his voice seemed different. There was a meanness—a shocking and cold malevolence to it—that was alarming and even a tad menacing.

He immediately began ripping into me about the football practice. How dare I show up there. How selfish I was to think I would ever be allowed to play football and ruin his team's chances to win the Tweaker Bowl. Why did I even bother, when I knew how bad I was?

"Gays don't play football," he screamed. "Why can't you just go do gay things and stop trying to be what you are not?"

I tried to explain that I had no intention of ruining anything for anyone, I just wanted to be a part of things, like the program said we should be.

"Plus, as my sponsor, aren't you supposed to push me outside my box?" I asked.

But he wasn't having it. He was out for blood. He had moved on to berating me for a meeting I had chaired. I'd lost that meeting because the halfway house that hosted it had decided to ban me form their property when I recommended a better place to people, in order to help them get sober. He told me I was the disgrace of our entire fellowship. Then he asked how I could be so stupid. How I could ever show my face again. Then he moved on to my bipolar diagnosis:

"You only use that as a crutch," he said, destroying me.

I've never used it as a crutch—or intended to. I only speak of it because others like me are afraid to do so and I want them to know there is nothing to be ashamed of. I want people like me to know that they can claim their power as well. It was all a little weird and a little too over the top. Sponsors are supposed to be forceful and tell it like it is, but they aren't supposed to make fun of you for having a disease or for not being good at sports because you're fat and gay.

By this time, he had broken me down to the point that I was gutturally sobbing. I was begging him to stop, actually. I didn't know where any of this was coming from. I had done everything in my power to be such a good boy. I had done everything in my power to honor him, to make him love me. But he didn't. It seemed like he actually hated me. He went on and on, and then his sinister tone turned inward:

"I don't know why you bother with a loser from the gutter like me," he said, sounding pained.

Sobbing, I begged him to stop saying things that weren't true. I tried my sparkle talk: "Don't you know how beautiful you are?" I begged. "Look at all you've overcome." But my kindness fell on deaf ears. He was done with me. And he was using the same language to get rid of me as he had done with my hot tub loving ex. He went at me so much that it triggered my PTSD, which had originally been caused by the abusive relationship I'd been in prior to Pack.

After a solid hour of screaming put-downs at me and belittling me to the point I felt like I was nothing, he said the words I thought would end me once and for all:

"You need to find a new sponsor."

He hung up on me. I cradled the phone, sobbing. I'm pretty sure I screamed "Noooooooooo" into it, like they do in the movies when someone dies in someone's arms. Only I was not Whitney Houston and he was most assuredly not my Bodyguard. He would definitely not always love me.

But there was no one there on the other end to hear my crying. And I knew I couldn't call the one person I thought I needed to make this pain go away. He had caused it! Any relationship with him was over. It was the end of *Dantrick*, and really, the world as I knew it. This was going to hurt. And did it ever.

There's a funny thing about endings, where I am concerned. Just like the last one, when Pack died and I thought my life was over, I quickly realized this ending was another beautiful beginning. This time, instead of depending on another man to save me or rescue me, I did it for myself and found a beautiful relationship with the only man who really matters. God. This is a relationship I now maintain and nurture through regular prayer and meditation.

The Sparkle King

Water from the Moon

There is a saying that if you focus on the hurt, you continue to suffer; but if you focus on the lesson, you will continue to grow.

Something about the way Daniel talked to me that night changed the way I would normally react to such a personal affront.

I'd like to say our separation was seamless, but it wasn't. We still were on several committees together and he was still in charge of all of them. So I would go and he would totally ignore me, which would cause me to act out in front of everyone, which would then cause him to respond by lashing out at me via text. He never once faced me and just talked to me like men are supposed to do.

At first, I thought the whole thing would blow over, so I just stopped responding to his outrageous texting outbursts. However, I was scheduled to chair the meeting at our fellowship's biggest event of the year on Halloween and Daniel and I were still not talking. I wasn't sure I wanted to put myself through the discomfort of facing him in front of the whole fellowship.

Everyone, including CP and Melissa, told me it would show major growth if I showed up in spite of his casual and increasingly agitated cruelty. It came down to the wire and I almost languished in my immature old ways as I considered avoiding the pain by not showing up. However, my new sponsor Reginald—a large black man who seemed menacing until you looked into his eyes and actually saw the comfort and power of God—told me I was going, no matter what. And so that was it.

So I did what I had never done before: I faced my fear, went to the event, and honored my commitment. I even wore a suit. Daniel ignored me at first but later spoke to me generically and even helped Melissa and I collect money for the event, which had made more cash than any other event in our fellowship's history. I noticed he was wearing the ring, which oddly comforted me. But when the event was over, he went back to being stone cold.

I decided I was just going to keep suiting up and showing up. But Daniel's behavior to me was not just cold, it was abusive. Also, he was treating me this way in front of everyone we knew. I've been in an abusive relationship before with a man—he had kicked me, spat on me, beaten me and yelled at me. In my sobriety though, I had gained self-esteem; I wouldn't allow it to continue. So I paused and prayed, asking for guidance on how to write a text that I was withdrawing from the committee without sounding whiny. And that is what I did.

Daniel's response to my thoughtful note, which was grateful and gracious, was venomous and hateful. He lashed out again. And I wasn't able to contain my hurt during our very last exchange. I told him he was not allowed to abuse me and that not only did I never want to speak to him again, I wanted my key back. He had a key to my apartment from when he had redone my living room and asking for it back seemed like the best way to one-up his malevolent cruelty.

You should always be careful what you ask for, because I got both my wishes: my key back and a vow of silence. I still see him a lot. We share friends, we are in the same men's group, and I even have to go to meetings at the halfway house where he is the manager. There is no eye contact when we pass each other. It's like I don't even exist. It's very immature on his part and speaks volumes about his character.

But you know what: for the first time in my life, I possess such a resolute personal power and love for myself that I don't care how others treat me. That's their stuff, not mine! The thing about people, places and things is that they will always do the things that people, places and things do. And I know I have no control over any of it. Happiness is an inside job. If I want to stay in the joy and grace of the miracle of life in sobriety, I have to manifest it for myself.

I've apologized since the melee for my part in it. I've prayed for him to have everything I want in life and everything he wants, as my sponsor suggested. I even reached out to him to wish him a happy sobriety birthday. Throughout this whole thing—the most painful thing I have endured in my entire sobriety—I have remained kind, loving, and I have lived in the solution. That's all I can do: focus on me.

I know I can't do anything about his reaction to me. He is going to do what he wants to do and for now, his choice is to act like I don't exist. And that's okay because my side of the street is clean and my willingness to push through this pain and fear has made me learn to rely on God for the first time in my life. That means that I am living in the miracle, as God's love is infinite and always there. He offers a welcoming safety and benevolent sanctuary that no human can.

I've chased men like Daniel since I was in junior high. And the results were always the same until now. However, this painful experience forced me to love myself more than ever. I even love him, in spite of his awful behavior to me. Whether or not he ever changes towards me—he still wears my ring, after all—I know this for sure: love always wins and I choose to love me.

The Sparkle King

How it Feels to Fly

In my early career, I was a journalist. I loved that work; meeting beautiful, interesting new people every day and getting to help them through painful periods in their life by finding the beauty in it, then writing articles that benefitted the community by informing them and helping them learn new things. I had gone far in that field, ultimately becoming the editor of the largest gay magazine in the Southwest Valley. It was there that I would interview celebrities like Katy Perry, Jennifer Hudson, and my favorite, Tori Spelling. But it was also there that my ego inflated so big that it had no other choice than to be brought down a few pegs by a man who beat and belittled me on a regular basis. My toxic relationship with my abuser made me feel I had lost control of myself, which ultimately made me lash out at others. Unfortunately, the wrong ones; I got fired from the most lucrative job I'd ever had because I mouthed off to my boss.

It was during the low of the next two years of unemployment, and the even deeper abyss of depression and uselessness that I felt as a result of the abuse, that I got the bright idea of putting an ad online to learn how to do drugs. It was there I met my future partner, Pack, who remains my greatest love and the cause of every blessing I've experienced since his sudden death. Yes, I can even find gratitude in being beaten to within an inch of my life because it led me to that love. Things look and feel different from a distance.

Not long after I'd met Pack, I started working for a huge hotel company. I worked there during the entirety of our all-too-short relationship and then all the way through the all-consuming grief caused by the sudden and unwelcome end of it.

Corporate jobs are interesting in that if your boss hires you, you're golden. The 'chosen one'. Many years of my seven-year tenure at this company were bliss, especially since I was the boss's favorite. But the minute he left—a few months after Pack's untimely exit—my cache dropped considerably. I don't think trying to fly out of a 26th story window in Vegas after a Mariah Carey concert while high on drugs really helped me; nor did the fact that I was completely open about being a gay, bipolar, drug addict widow abuse survivor. I was who I was and I was not afraid of it, even though it seemed everyone else was.

The other thing about Corporate America is that if you are the golden child, the sky's the limit. There are plenty of people who dream about climbing the corporate ladder. I am not one of them. That doesn't mean I don't want to grow and change and try new things; it just means the grandiose scale of how big, important and immediate everything was in that over-the-top environment wasn't anywhere near the truth of who I was.

I love people. I love getting to know them. I yearn for intimacy; connection. I want to make the world a better place, swim with dolphins, feed the children, and spread the love. I do not want to be limited by numbers and quotas. I do not want to have to pretend to be cutthroat and hard, when all I really want to do is look you in the eye and learn about who you are.

Another issue with that job was that at the end of the day, I reported up through a labyrinthine maze of five bosses. Every word I wrote—every sentence, every thought—was poured over and manipulated and discussed and dissected and destroyed. One person would like it, but the next wouldn't. Then another would want to go in an entirely different direction. And none of it was communicated very well. From my perspective, I didn't feel like I could get any work done. Ultimately, I also didn't feel valued—even though two of those bosses had come to my first book's opening gala and had even read the damn thing. I just knew the writing was on the wall.

The tension and anxiety this job created made it feel like I was in jail every day, serving a life sentence. Though I had been diagnosed bipolar, I was on five anxiety and anti-depressants at the end of my time there, which seems like overkill, since I'm now only on two as a result of daily prayer and meditation. I routinely felt like I was on the verge of a heart attack: I could feel hands pressing down on me as I sat at my desk. I felt pangs of intense dread; the fear was practically eating away at my soul, which felt dead. I left there many days in tears, going home to sit in a coma of fear and terror.

I felt stuck. The money was amazing and I was comfortable. It was safe. I had already been totally crazy pants and was known for it, therefore I knew I'd never get fired—which had been an overwhelming fear of mine since being fired from the magazine.

Then, in addition to the hands choking me, I began to hear it—it was a whisper. It told me if I had the courage to walk away from this job I hated, I would be rewarded for choosing faith over fear. This voice seemed trustworthy and close—I know now it was coming from the God inside me. However, at that time I would think about finances and I would succumb to the hands pressing against my flesh. No, I couldn't leave. Not today, Satan.

My sponsor asked me to pray about it. Specifically, he asked me to ask for a sign. And then, much like the Vegas debacle, I got hit with a 2x4: I calmly and professionally attempted to tell my boss about a situation that I was having trouble with. I asked her to help me with it. She shot up in her chair and shot a sharp, daggered look at me that I had never seen in her usually kind eyes.

"You're attacking me!" she said.

"No, no, I'm not," I begged.

I started to cry. I knew I was being misunderstood that day, but to put a word like that around any of my behavior cut to the core. I wasn't that kind of person and it just wasn't true. I knew deep down I couldn't accept this affront to my character, even though I had done in the past during similar situations.

I left the room sobbing the hardest I had done since finding Pack dead. The first thing I did was call HR. Then I called my sponsor and, through broken heaves, I relayed to him what had happened to me. But then I surprised myself: instead of going home like HR had told me I could, I went back and faced the situation as Reginald had suggested. HR told me we could address everything on the following Monday. I agreed to let things simmer down over the weekend. I had been in and out of HR repeatedly in the past and while they always put a band-aid on the situation, this time it felt different to me. A line had been crossed. I'm not an aggressive person. I'm loving and soft to the very core of my being. However, my 'whisper' was now rolling its eyes at me.

That weekend, Reginald and I had to drive to an out of town leadership event for our fellowship in Tucson. As we talked, I shared what had happened and suddenly, he delivered words I desperately wanted to hear:

"When a situation feels so uncomfortable that you feel you have no other choice but to leave, it's a sign from God that it is time for you go."

I'm glad he said it. I had been wanting to get out of there for a long time and now—finally—I had someone supporting me. Not only that, my sponsor is deeply spiritual, so I knew his revelation coupled with that nagging whisper from within and the invisible hands clenching around my throat meant it was time to spread my wings.

Even though I couldn't see the whole staircase, I suddenly had enough faith to know that if I left there, I was going to be okay. God had a plan for me! We agreed that at the planned tête-a-tête with HR and my bosses on the following Monday—which also happened to be my former abuser's birthday and the one-year anniversary of the release of my book—I would finally resign.

On that day, I allowed myself to be free; I wore a suit. I walked into the conference room with a smile on my face. I looked all of my leaders in the eye and then I became one. I sat up in my chair and spoke powerfully about how I was thankful for the opportunity and that I had learned a lot. Then I explained that I was not being true to myself by continuing to stay there and that it was time for me to let go, as I deserved to be happy and chase my dreams.

When I was done speaking, I looked around the room. Everyone was smiling. I think there might have even been clapping—not because I had been brave enough to resign but because I had so lovingly and authoritatively taken back the narrative of my life and stopped being a victim. They respected me and they were proud of me. For the first time in nearly seven years, I actually did climb the corporate ladder—by jumping off of it.

Then another miracle happened: I wasn't escorted out of the building. For almost seven years, my biggest fear had been that I would be fired and thrown away like I had been the last time. But these people I spent several years in fear of finally liked me. They asked me if I would give two weeks' notice and sent loving, congratulatory, proud e-mails to other bosses about how I was leaving to follow my dreams. I even got a going away party!

Then, on the last day, when I finally stepped out of my comfort zone and into the miracle on the other side, I looked at my phone. An old journal entry had popped up on my phone when I wasn't touching it—a note I believed came from my dead lover. It read: "It's over."

And it was. I got in my car and drove away. I immediately noticed the license plate in front of me read

"Butterfly." And yes, just like Mariah sings, it was time for me to spread my wings and prepare. Because this was what it felt like to fly.

Bang, Bang

My love life since Pack died has been as barren and dry as the desert I live in.

There was one guy I liked that I used to use drugs with. However, he cheated on me right in front of my face by leaving with someone we had invited over. Then there was the whole *"that I used to use with"* part of that sentence, which also made him a solid no for me. Then there was *hot tub guy*, who has been loaded for the majority of the two years since we broke up and was only just getting clean. His inability to stay sober—not to mention the whole hot tub fiasco—took him off the leader board.

And then there was Skip, a somewhat mysterious trucker who was also a sober widow. I had found him on Facebook through his comments on a mutual friend's post. I Facebook stalked him and was immediately drawn to him because he wrote beautiful posts about his dead lover. I felt a kinship to him because I still write beautiful posts about Pack too.

I friended him and we became "friends." He often liked my posts—especially my increasingly spiritual ones—and eventually, we started talking. He didn't live here in Phoenix but had done so once, with his now dead partner. He still came here from time to time because he was a trucker and often had downtime. Also, he missed the outdoor activities he enjoyed here, like four-wheeling and hiking.

We harmlessly went along for months just liking each other's posts and chatting briefly every now and again via messenger. It didn't seem likely this flame would ignite—he was still in love with his partner and had not moved through his grief, even though he said he'd had eleven years of sobriety. The truth is, all these years later, I'm still in love with Pack too.

But then one day he literally showed up out of nowhere.

"Would we be able to get together?" he asked.

I really couldn't. I had plans to go to the movies with Daniel that night and I wasn't about to miss out on time with him! However, this guy I had a cyber crush on was finally here, so I agreed to meet him for coffee prior to going to Daniel's.

And so I finally met Skip. He was a little geekier than I imagined—he always looked so rugged and masculine in all his outdoorsy Facebook posts. However, he was immediately funny—charming even—and even better, there was an energy about him that seemed safe.

Coffee was enjoyable so we decided to go antiquing. I was starting to get nervous—I really was having a good time but I had to get to Daniel's to keep my plans with him. So I asked him to come with me. Yes, on my first date in over a year since the hot tub massacre, I basically took my new suitor over to my daddy's house for his approval. I could tell they were totally oblivious to each other, and I could also feel a chemistry growing with Skip that would be hampered by being around Daniel and his clique. So I shocked myself and agreed to skip my plans with Daniel—*gasp!*—and go on a movie date with Skip. And it was great. I had a good time, and the conversation was light and fun. I hoped I would see him again.

But then we went back to our innocent Facebook flirtation. Several weeks passed. It didn't seem like he was coming back to Phoenix. Then he again just showed up out of nowhere. This time he had the whole weekend off and he decided to "surprise me."

Then he asked: "Can I stay with you?"

I was okay with it—I was glad he was here again. It seemed romantic and spontaneous and exciting. And that second experience was all of that—well, maybe not romantic.

He left, again unable to pinpoint when he would be back. But then, a few weeks later, he just showed up again on my doorstep. Though it was slightly annoying and even a bit creepy if I am being honest, I was in full-on 'like' with this dude and given everything we had in common on paper, I had convinced myself he was *the one*. This was despite the fact it was clear he was not over his dead lover, nor did he participate in his sobriety. We never went anywhere near sex.

This time was also different in that because of a prior speeding ticket he had just been made aware of, he couldn't work until it got squared away. It might be at least four days, maybe a week until he could get on the road again. Could he stay again? Of course.

By this time, Daniel and I were done and my tenure at my job was about to end. I had called in sick because Daniel and I had just had our final and most deadly encounter, the one where I asked for the key back. A nice day trip with Skip was just the medicine I needed. He would take me to Globe—the very spot CP and I would spend a relaxing, jovial day antiquing and becoming best friends several months later—and we would eat at his favorite Mexican spot.

So we got in the car and just drove. It was a wonderful, relaxing, easy day. We were totally vibing. However, we still weren't banging and I was getting a little annoyed about that, not that I was doing anything to make it happen either.

I was telling everyone he was the one, maybe because I needed someone to make me feel safe again after my blow-out with the man who had been my primary caretaker. But it was all still very platonic. Then the bottom fell out and things got weird.

He had asked me to go to church with him on a Sunday morning. I told him I couldn't because I was going shopping for Melissa's birthday present with CP. Somehow he hadn't heard me—or he was looking for a fight. I think the latter. The whole thing got so out of control and messy.

When I got home from shopping with CP, he still wasn't home. And then all the batshit crazy texting started. Skip was pissed that I had ignored him and skipped church. He was sending me text after text from some undisclosed location, sounding madder with each one and a little menacing too, if I am being honest. This went on for three hours but I had an *a-ha* moment in the midst of it—so I finally told Skip I had feelings for him! I thought the issue was the murky, unsettled, *are we or aren't we* vibe and that if I told him how I felt, he would melt. You would have thought my bold, brave declaration would have changed the dynamic. I'm pretty sure if someone told me they had feelings for me I would stop being a little bitch and like them back. But that's just me.

He did finally come home, but he was cold and distant. He remained that way the next day too, to the point that I felt uncomfortable in my own home. I was upset because we had made plans for dinner but I had seen him post on social media that he was already at dinner while I was on my way home from work. When he finally got home, way past the dinner hour, I asked how this misunderstanding was any different from the one about church the day before. I told him that I could move past it because it was a miscommunication but then he just got upset about the church again and started another fight about it. As such, I left my house angry.

I called Reginald and CP after I stormed out of my own house. Both were shocked I was spending this much energy on someone I wasn't banging. My sponsor told me I should ask him to leave, but I didn't think that was a very nice thing to do. So I did what I do now when I have a problem I can't solve on my own: I got on my knees before God, humbled myself, and ask him to show me a sign.

I awoke the next morning and Skip had left without leaving any kind of communication about where he was going. I felt terrified about doing anything because every time I did, I was accused of ignoring him and being the worst, most awful, no-good person who had ever lived. And we weren't even banging—have I mentioned that?

Then he burst through my door and I got my sign from God. About a minute into his return we—still not banging!—were arguing again. He said the meanest thing I think anyone has ever said to me:

"Now I understand why Pack was high all the time. He had to be in order to be around you."

I shot up from the couch. "Oh, is that how you feel?" I asked. Rage was building inside me.

"Yes, you are really hard to be around. I feel sorry for Pack."

And then I did what I have never done before when a man abused me, verbally or otherwise: I demanded he left my home.

"If that's how you feel, the door is that way."

He looked shocked and stood in front of me, frozen. I think he was surprised at my sudden and resolute strength and power.

"Oh, is that what you want?" he asked.

"Yes you ungrateful user, get out of my house now." He shot me a single pained expression, as if he was trying to murder me with his eyes in the same way he had just done with his words.

I stood up and walked toward him. "What's taking you so long?" I asked.

And then, just like that, he was gone. I locked the door behind him and I leaned back in my couch, feeling relieved. I think I expected I would cry, but instead I blocked him on my phone and social media and felt prouder of myself than I had ever done.

For the first time in my life, I had stopped a man from abusing me. Yes, God and I had done it yet again. We had set me free from the cycle of abuse within a single and resounding bang.

The Sparkle King

Ego

If I had the opportunity to speak with Daniel today, I would say two simple words to him: thank you. I'd also attempt to make my part in the dissolution of our relationship right, although that is what I have always done. However, because he won't speak to me, he has no idea how grateful I am. I owe him a huge debt of gratitude because his sudden disowning of me forced me to deal with the root cause of more than forty years of issues I'd had with men like him.

To put it simply, I have daddy issues. This was coupled with my ego, which was so afraid of success that it forced me to cower behind Daniel. It made me hide the beautiful sparkle I had unearthed for myself in sobriety. I went backward because my ego was trying to sabotage me. Not only was I 'safe' from any type of success, but Daniel's cache in our community also made it look like I was thriving—as long as I was standing next to him, it appeared that I was. I also didn't have to deal with men because I made him my own—I really have not approached a man as a 'man' on any level since Pack died. On top of this, I didn't have to grow spiritually because Daniel made for a great spiritual stand-in. Daniel was like a band-aid for everything that ailed me.

I believe God made it rain and forced a flood because He knew it was time for me to grow into the man I was supposed to be. Love increases when your ego is less invested. God knew I needed to step out of fear and judgement, and into my unlimited, higher self. It would be the only way that I could open myself up to love as a force of nature. Now I am basking in that harvest—that love. I can even see flowers starting to grow in the once barren and muddy earth that once almost swallowed me whole.

A life lived in love is the most realistic life of all. So it took Daniel dumping me, a career shake-up, a man I thought I was going to fall in love with turning on me, and a shady publicist stopping my literary momentum to get me humbled enough to finally seek out the only love that matters: the one through God, that is found by getting on my knees every day and asking for it.

Now that I am here, I have opened myself up to love in a way that I never thought was possible. Because in this beautiful space, I feel Him working for me and through me. I have grown more in these last six months than I have in my whole life.

One great thing about God is He doesn't make you do anything by yourself. He leads you to the people you need to find; those that will help you find Him. I feel the loving electricity, spiritual tenacity and immediate force of God in my new sponsor, Reginald. It feels like every word that comes out of his mouth is from God. I know that when Reginald speaks, I had better listen and follow suit if I want to grow.

God also has a sense of humor. Daniel was always on my case about my sloppy appearance. I think he felt that what I looked like rubbed off on him in some way. As such, he forced me to dress a certain way, to let him redo my living room, and insisted I got my car detailed every month.

I know the last part is a direct intervention from God because I also know how my dead lover felt about a clean car. Early in our relationship—before long-term drug use made me act callous, crude and sometimes verbally hateful toward him—we had this beautiful day in the sun where we both spent several sober hours together in my parents' driveway, washing our cars. For some reason, Pack loved this day. He animatedly spoke of it throughout the entirety of our too-short relationship. He always wanted to recreate the magic, but I wasn't into it—it was work. One of the first psychic mediums I ever spoke to after his death told me that Pack was urging me from beyond the grave to keep my car clean. She said it was the most insistent thing he kept repeating.

I would have ignored this advice if it hadn't been for Daniel being so set in his ways about outward appearance and pushy about his expectations. As an only child, I never learned the value of cleaning because my mother practically walked three steps behind me my entire life, cleaning up after me. It should be noted, I didn't move out of home until I was thirty-seven. I've also never been much of a fashion plate. I'm a fat, middle-aged man. I seriously doubt anyone really looks at what I'm wearing—except for the shoes. The over-the-top, light-shifting magnificent sparkle of them tells you who I really am and how I feel about myself.

One of the blessings of 12-step programs is that just about everyone I know has some kind of specific skill that they do for a job, and these come in very handy. I knew Reginald because he was an amazing event planner for the fellowship. He always seemed to pull me aside and give me tips so that I could grow with the responsibilities I was getting as I attained more sobriety. I did not realize it early on—I actually was annoyed, the way I always am when anyone tries to tell me anything true about me—but Reginald took an interest in my development as a spiritual human being.

Daniel was only concerned about what I looked like on the surface. Reginald always pulled the insides of me to the outside, and still does. And wouldn't you know what he does for a living—he is a car detailer. Yes, my dead lover knew who the right one was all along. I just had to figure it out for myself.

My personal relationship with Reginald actually began when he came over to wash and detail my car because Daniel had made me do it. The fissure in my relationship with Daniel was already there, but I was desperately trying to stop our earth from moving further apart because my ego felt safe there. However, as

Reginald worked on my car, I'd increasingly go outside earlier and earlier to talk to him. Where Daniel was always closed off, surly and often shut me down, Reginald listened intently for meaning and asked probing questions that made me search deeper within, helping me get to the root cause of things. I didn't know it early on, but his low-key spiritual juju that came from the pit of his soul was working its way through me, even in those early days.

Once Daniel and I had the final texting massacre, I asked Reginald if he would be my sponsor. He was honored. Then the real work began. I couldn't make any more excuses, or hide behind my ego or my self-sabotaging antics anymore, because Reginald just wasn't having it. He is so spiritual—so deeply intuitive—that sometimes I feel like he knows what I am going to say before even I do. Sometimes he says a version of it and then, twenty minutes later, I say the same thing.

Early on in this sponsorship, he told me that my loneliness—all that despair I felt that led me to Daniel in the first place—was a spiritual issue. While it was a feat that I had multiple years of sobriety, the only way I was going to keep them and get more of them—and be happy, joyous and free—would be to get to work on finding real, solid, unbreakable emotional sobriety.

And so we began the work. And I will say this: I've worked harder and given up more of myself and the bad character defects that I had than with any other man in my life. Because of Reginald, I found God. This singular mighty force in my life, sent to me by God and my partner, changed a habit I'd had for forty-three years: chasing the wrong men for love, safety and security. Now I could plant myself in the loving arms of the only man that matters—God. And that is a miracle. Which means I need to thank Daniel for getting out of the way so I could find the love I deserved.

Faith

The moment you make a decision to do something you really want, the whole universe rushes to be on your side.

Some call it the law of attraction. I call it a divinely-inspired 'a-ha moment,' where we follow the whisper inside our soul to the path our intuition has led us toward. In many cases, this requires the faith of a mustard seed—or at least enough to take the first step, even if you can't see the whole staircase.

It is in this beautiful moment we intuitively choose faith over fear. We step through that fear and past our comfort zone, into the magic and miracles on the other side. They only manifest if you work for them. And what I have learned is the harder we work in the direction of our goals—our destiny—the faster God and his angels conspire to make our dreams come true.

Here I was on the other side of the corporate ladder, having finally climbed it by being brave enough to jump off of it, and I knew I wanted to help people. I also knew that I wasn't going to settle until I found a job I really wanted, where I was able to do that. I didn't necessarily know what that looked like, or that there was a whole career field where I could do just this, but I had taken the first step.

God would immediately and readily fill in the staircase for me as I continued to take each new step.

The first thing that happened in a series of uncanny and divinely-timed events was that my former sponsor, Bill, told me the company he worked at held peer support classes. He thought I would be good at the work, so he suggested I came to his office and learned more. Though Bill and I have had our ups and downs, and it was the one-time failure of our relationship that made God lead me to Daniel, Bill had helped me more than anyone in my sobriety. First, he lovingly paraded me around the fellowship and introduced me to hundreds of people who instantly became beloved friends and soul mates. Now he was about to open the door to the career of my dreams with a suggestion based on his knowledge of who I really was at my core.

So with little information, I took the first step toward my new career in peer support. This field in behavioral health is relatively new, but in it, I get to help people like me work toward what they want. I do this through deep and loving communication, shared experiences and goal setting. It's kind of like being a therapist, only you don't have to go to school for fourteen years. Even better, you are on equal footing with someone. Nobody is better or above anyone. We work through things by sharing common experiences, helping each other grow through mutuality. It's a pretty amazing field actually.

I signed up for the class, which turned out to be exactly what I needed. It gave me a nice break between the drudgery of corporate America and the joy of finally stepping into the field of behavioral health where I belong.

The interesting thing about peer support is you have to be a drug addict or mentally ill to do it. So not only was I not going to be punished for being myself anymore, like I felt I was in the real world, I had to be real. It's a perfect job for an unapologetically gay, overweight, bipolar, drug addict, alcoholic widow abuse survivor in a pair of over-the-top sparkly shoes.

That doesn't mean I settled into it easily. I'm going to be honest, in my head I'm the most high-functioning bipolar person ever. Plus, daily meditation and prayer—not to mention not doing meth every day—have like, totally calmed me down. So when I walked in the room and saw a motley crew of real, in-the-flesh people living with mental illness, the fear that rules my ego made me think: "Oh, hell to the no! I'm not this bad!"

But then I remembered the last time Bill had put me into a situation that I went into kicking and screaming—my beloved men's group. I spent a whole month trying to get out of that, but something bigger than me—God—kept me going to it. Those men have become the closest friends I have ever had, the foundation of my sober life. It is through them I have grown into a real, bonafide man.

So instead of throwing a fit like I did the last time, I stayed there, sat down and started learning. Soon these people I had maligned with instant judgement started growing before my eyes. These beautiful, brave human beings began sharing their heart-breaking stories and opening themselves up in a way that made me see God inside them. And when you see God in someone, it shuts down the ego and reminds you to be careful about rash judgements. It also reminds you that people are a mirror; the things you fear in others are really what you fear in yourself.

Soon these people were my friends—lost souls who came together for six weeks to become something different and magical and whole. That time is now perhaps the most beautiful and memorable in my life. A time when about fourteen people who were once at their own rock-bottom formed a cocoon of love, emerging as glorious butterflies with new skills that they never imagined possible. We were ready to take the world on.

And this is the truth: I felt God the whole time I was there, so I knew it was going to work out. God even showed off a little during this time and I never sweated it. This was quite different from the boy who fell apart and became a raging drug addict the last time he hadn't been working full-time.

One day, Reginald told me I was going with him and other members of our men's group to help build a house in Mexico.

"But I need to look for a job," I said. The trip was the weekend before my graduation.

The Sparkle King

"You aren't going to do anything before you do this," he demanded.

My hesitation was really fear. What the hell did I know about building a house in Mexico? I don't build houses, I go to Britney Spears concerts.

But I didn't have to wonder for long. I surprised myself like I often do nowadays and went on the trip. As we began working on its foundation, I found myself floundering amid all my friends who were more "masculine" and who seemed more equipped for construction-related projects than I did.

I was very frustrated and close to giving up when my eyes became transfixed on a shiny white substance that looked like a cross between my two favorite accouterments: feathers and sparkle.

You see, foundations need dirt, water, concrete and just the right amount of fiberglass to hold a house together. I soon found myself sprinkling a little fiberglass into every wheelbarrow full of mix.

Soon, people complimented my flair and I didn't feel awful or frustrated. I didn't want to give up any more: I wanted to work harder and keep sprinkling my sparkle into the mix. I learned again, through that experience, that I could do things I thought I couldn't. All I had to do was remain true to myself, and make things my own.

The rest of the trip was just as magical. It felt like I could do anything. And the truth is, you really can when you step into the flow—when you are aware that you are doing everything in concert with God, the universe, and the beautiful plan for your life that was chosen by Him. It capped a week of staggering growth for me. I pushed through a lot of fear to let God manifest real miracles in my life.

On that Tuesday, I passed the Arizona state peer support exam with a one-hundred percent score.

On that Wednesday, I became American Red Cross certified in CPR and life-saving skills.

By Thursday, I was on my way to Mexico.

Three years ago, when I was slave to a meth pipe on

my closet floor, pushing a towel against the crack of light at the bottom so that no one would know what I was doing, I would never have envisioned any of this. If I am being honest, I wouldn't have even imagined this after I had been sober for a year.

But because I let go and let God lead the way, this is where I am and this is what I am doing now. I am doing things I couldn't have ever done, and discovering more about who I really am in the process. And you can do so too, when you let go and step out of fear and into faith. Do this and you will find the freedom you deserve.

I returned home from this life-affirming—and changing—trip and celebrated my graduation with those beautiful people who became mirrors into my own mental illness. The next day, I had an interview for a job as a behavioral health technician at a new all-men's rehab that was being opened by one of the leaders in my men's group. The next day I was hired. And just like that—because I was in the flow and pushed through my fear—I went from a boy who was afraid of men to someone who let a group of them love him. By doing this, I could become a man who leads other men into recovery and beyond. It's pretty powerful what God will do for you when you follow His whisper.

A few weeks later, I had orientation for my first job in recovery. I had dreamed of this moment for years.

I instantly felt the camaraderie, respect and love from my new work family. There was a sense of belonging and being needed and wanted that was so lacking in my last job.

Beyond that, I personally felt this overwhelming sense of love, gratitude and grace for God, as he had made this happen for me.

I remembered that, just a few short months ago, my fear and need to control my life had put me in the very same shackles I denounced when I got sober. I marveled at my willingness to step out of that fear and follow the whisper I had heard. This led me in the direction of my dreams.

Then I realized that because I let go and let God in, I was living a life beyond one I could have ever planned. That's what God does when you choose faith over fear.

That is, until He forces another flood to move you into the life that you really deserve.

Bombastic Love

Even in long-term sobriety, I've discovered—okay, Reginald told me—that I still have a lot of issues.

In the program, we call them character defects. For me, they are more like bombs that I create and then send some poor unknowing soul to detonate for me, because I want to be loved. I want to be seen as nice. *"You're gonna love me,"* Effie sings in *Dreamgirls*. And you better! I am the Sparkle King, after all. I have an image to maintain.

The problem with this is that the Sparkle King is just an alter ego, a character, a manifestation of who I really want to be. Patrick Roland is not the Sparkle King. It was Reginald that pointed that out. And it was because I finally stopped trying to live up to the expectations that the Sparkle King promised—and let God, the real and only Sparkle King, do it—that I could let myself be me and could finally grow into that role.

A great example of how cunning, baffling and manipulative I can be, occurred recently. I was co-chairing a meeting in a hospital with a friend named Kurt. I also happen to be very close to Mary, the girl he was dating at the time. She had let it slip in our group chat that Kurt was drinking. Not using drugs—but drinking every now and again.

I was outraged! I was offended! I was going to get to the bottom of this and make sure Kurt was penalized for his errant behavior. I also thought I was going to set someone else up to take the fall, because that shit gets messy and I'm so not messy!

I'm so glad God always knows better. He humbled me so I could finally learn from my errant ways and change for the better.

The Sparkle King

I went to Jimmy, the person who heads hospital meetings in our fellowship. I was all "I just can't believe Kurt is drinking" and "Whatever shall I do?" Then I sat back, grabbed some popcorn, and waited for my new reality show to unfold. If it worked in my favor, as it usually did, Jimmy would take the fall and no one would ever know I had said anything to anyone. I could get a sober co-chair and feel better about myself for being such an upstanding member of our community. Kurt and I could still be friends and he'd never know I was his saboteur! Sounds like I unabombed the shit out of that one, right?

I had, until the bomb I constructed went off on Facebook while I was taking the state peer support exam I needed to pass for the new career I had chosen after bravely leaving my corporate job. I had just finished taking the test—I got one-hundred percent—when I found my phone was a mess of angry texts from Kurt. Even worse, a dialogue about the situation was unspooling on Facebook.

"Don't you people know how I feel about being portrayed on Facebook," I said to myself, rolling my eyes and feeling so bothered that these people were doing this to *me*.

So, what, did I pause when agitated? No. Did I pray? No. I jumped right in and poured gasoline all over the bitch and then acted surprised when it blew up in my face.

Jimmy had asked on Facebook what should happen if the chair of a hospital meeting was found to be drinking. Kurt saw it and knew it was about him. He then resigned from the chair position of the meeting. Then he went off on me—rightly so—for not bothering to talk to him about it in person. So what did I do? I claimed moral outrage and pointed the finger at Jimmy.

"How dare you post this on Facebook," I yelled. "This was a personal issue. Anyone with half a brain doesn't post stuff like this on social media. It's an anonymous program, dumbass." And then I clutched my pearls for emphasis and went in on Jimmy, basically deriding his whole character in a series of my now famous, cleverly-worded insults. It seemed to work in my favor—everyone on Facebook still liked me—phew!—and Jimmy looked like a moron. Winner!

I was right about one thing—it was a personal issue. The truth is, I made this whole thing happen—and at the most stressful possible time, I might add—because I was too chicken and too desperate to be loved to be able to have a simple conversation with my friend. Even though I actually loved him.

Even worse, I had seen Kurt in person twice since I had talked to Jimmy about his 'sins.' I knew he was going to be asked to step down from his gig, and I said nothing on either occasion. Two days before Jimmy detonated the bomb, I sat at a dinner table with Kurt and Mary and noted to both of them that he seemed down.

"He's afraid you told on him and that he is going to lose his meeting," Mary said when I asked. And still, the 'Sparkle King' sat there and said nothing. I'm pretty sure I just changed the conversation, even though her words ate away at me.

Now that I've made amends with both men, I have realized that this situation wasn't all that different from all the other 'crises' in my life that I've caused. However, I now approach things differently: by addressing them when they happen instead of allowing my fear to cause them to spiral out of control. The truth is, I am the common denominator and the main cause of all that ails me when I fail to bring God into the picture.

For example, I was having a hard time with life recently.

For a good portion of the day, I pushed through crippling anxiety and fear. I don't have these panic attacks often anymore because of my commitment to the stillness and awareness that meditation brings, but when I do, it seems impossible to stop them.

I was manically cleaning out my car—throwing

things, cussing, losing my shit on errant Diet Coke cans that fell out because I hadn't thrown them away in the first place. Again, a problem of my creation, as they all are.

And then a single white feather fell to the ground in front of me. I knew it was God and my angels reminding me that everything was going to be okay. So instead of freaking out, falling apart, or setting up someone to take the fall for me, I stopped and prayed.

Again, God, the real and true Sparkle King, did what only he can do—he made everything okay in my world so that I could sparkle again. And not only do I do that, I actually now face problems before they detonate. Like I did recently, with my father.

Against All Odds

Every day when I walk my dogs, I look for feathers at the dog park.

Usually, a feather initially proves elusive. But then, I see one fluttering at me as if it's saying hello. Then—just like that—I see two and then three. Suddenly, all I see is feathers everywhere.

I've realized this experience is a metaphor for awareness. It is when I look closer and allow myself to be exactly in this moment, concentrating on what I want, I am able to manifest everything I am looking for.

Through meditation, where I really connect with my inner whisper—my intuition—I've been able to manifest dreams I never thought would materialize. Whether it's my ability to forgive and pray for people who have wronged me, or the ease in which I move past things that once would have been the end of me, this awareness, this ability to stay in the flow, has altered me dramatically.

Any one of the things that happened to me last fall — the Daniel fallout, the break up with the bad guy, the job stress, or the dishonest publicist—would have undone me in the past. As a matter of fact, these are exactly the things that led me to post an ad on the Internet looking for someone to teach me to do drugs. But now, because I live in a constant state of flow—a peaceful energy that is led by God and that propels me to my higher self— these roadblocks no longer get in my way. I have consistently chosen faith over fear and I can see the results; there is a proven track record from God that He will always show up so that I can show up for myself. I can now easily traverse anything that tries to knock me out of the flow. Yes, Donkey Kong is still throwing his barrels at me. But now, instead of jumping over them, I'm floating in a state of airy bliss that I have attained through this constant zen-like state of awareness and appreciation for everything that is happening to me right now.

That doesn't mean I don't have bad days or even the rushed, disturbed, crazy thoughts I always have had whilst living with my bipolar; it just means I find it easier to manage my symptoms.

For example, I overslept recently because I was having my recurring dream in which I am a Kardashian. This set off a chain reaction of everything else going wrong.

My headphones weren't charged so I couldn't meditate. The dogs were overwhelming. I knocked a cup over. I dropped my phone in between my seat and the console in my car.

THE WORLD WAS ENDING. I WAS A LOSER. MY LIFE SUCKED.

Then I opened up Instagram and the first thing I saw was a post by Eckhart Tolle reminding me that I was not my thoughts, which was the same Oprah and Deepak meditation I had been listening to the night before. I got in my car later and *"The Blood,"* a BeBe & CeCe Winans song about God, came on the radio. Suddenly, a car drove by with the letters *'NLV'* on it, which is a type of Bible. And then another car drove by with the license plate *'KimmieK,'* referencing my favorite Kardashian, which brought me right back to my dreams earlier that day.

Then I realized that I was exactly where I was supposed to be. My life was actually in flow with the universe and I was not my thoughts. I am so far from those things because I am actually completely aligned with God, and that just may mean I really am a Kardashian after all. Or else maybe I'm about to achieve a level of success similar to theirs, as I know dreams are really just a series of symbols that I am able to tune into now.

One of the most important lessons I have taken away from becoming one with the flow is: You are not your thoughts. All those things you are telling yourself right now—that you are not enough; that you can't do this, you won't do that—are a lie. I know for sure you ARE enough, you CAN, and you WILL. Because if I can do things like help my friends build a house for charity change careers in my early forties, or even successfully go camping, then you can too. Stop listening to the voices inside your head that are full of lies. Instead, start listening—become one—with the voice inside your heart. This voice is your truth that walks you through the maze of your fears, past the lazy, hazy bliss of your comfort zone and into the magic where life really begins.

It is here in this beautiful, majestic, space of light and love that you can awaken to the awareness of your ego trying to waste your time. It is also here that you can discover life in the flow—in the truth of God and Source—where you belong.

The Sparkle King

Ambitions

The stove clock said 11:11.

I closed my eyes and said a prayer to my favorite angel, my dead partner.

"Pack, will you show me a sign that I am going to manifest my goal of getting my work all the way to Oprah?"

Then suddenly, out of nowhere—in my kitchen, in my apartment that he never set foot in alive—a single white feather showed up at my feet, answering "yes."

This kind of thing happens all the time, almost daily. My lover may have fallen to the ground in death, but he never left my side. He still sends messages through songs—and now, more often feathers—to say hello and remind me of his love.

For example, when I was in Mexico building a house recently, I sensed the heralding of a miracle when I noticed a beautiful single white feather as it leisurely fell to my feet.

The thing is, the dry, barren Mexican desert where I had been building a house isn't a hot spot for such a bird that would produce a feather like this—so where did it come from?

And because I can't answer that logically, I have to choose faith and believe that it's Pack sending me a perfectly timed message from God, telling me that His big beautiful plan for my life is unfolding and manifesting as it should. This feather intuitively told me that if I continue to choose faith over fear, if I continue to grow in gratitude and grace for my many blessings that I am already aware of, it will. Because I believe today that miracles can and will happen if I stay in prayer and meditation, if I trust the process, and if I stay close to God.

Examples of this happen all the time. I know I'm about to manifest success because I will spot a feather and then out of nowhere, my phone will seemingly rise from the dead and start playing BeBe & CeCe Winans' "*Hold Up the Light*" when I am not touching it. I sense from my intuition that this is really a symbol for my sparkle—my brand—which I believe is going to set the world on fire.

Suddenly, as if Pack and God are answering me, the song switches without me touching it to Whitney Houston's "*Million Dollar Bill*"—because my faith tells me if I keep doing what I am doing and sharing my light—my brilliant, beautiful, breathtaking sparkle—with the world, I will manifest success beyond my wildest dreams. That may very well be why I keep dreaming I am a Kardashian after all.

The next day, I ask Pack: "What did you mean when you played those two songs for me yesterday? Later, the phone 'comes alive' again in my pocket. I pull it out of my shorts. He answers me. "*Believe*" by Cher is now playing, in the same way these three songs always do.

The power of his eternal and undying love moves me to my core—I sense Pack is in a different place now than before. I know he has made it to heaven and I know he stays close because he is an angel now. A beautiful, resilient angel who sits at the feet of God, sending the love of his life songs and feathers. He does this to remind me that if I continue to believe—and follow my intuition through prayer and meditation—I'm going to make it, in the way he always knew I would.

From the very first night we met, he played a song for me called "*Ambitions*" by Joe McElderry. It stated that "*If somebody was gonna make it, that somebody outta be me.*" I now believe that Pack was speaking words of prophecy when he picked that song for me—I just had to follow God's Plan and spend my time in the dark so I could make it into the light. It's the same type of faith or prophecy that I believe was spoken from my friend Mike, who was another beautiful angel sent to me by God. A god that loves and protects me by pushing me toward these people, so that I can share their last moments with them.

As Mike lay dying from cancer, halfway between this world and the one he now shares with Pack, he introduced me to his family.

"This is my friend, Patrick. He's just written a book and he's going to make it all the way to Oprah." I believe he said that because the angel pulling him toward heaven told him it.

And so I stay in the flow, following the signs my dead loved ones continue to send from Heaven—because our soul can always feel the energy of our departed loved ones. They are now wild and free like all the best things are, but their spirits—their love for us—is very much here with us. Because God doesn't want us to be lonely so he sends them back to us as angels. We just have to move past the fear that this isn't possible and into the faith that proves it is, over and over again.

Another example of this occurred when had dinner with six of my friends recently, a table full of dudes. We were celebrating CP's birthday.

I sat there and I remembered that little kid I used to be, who was beaten up and called names by men. I remember that kid wishing—praying?—to be loved, accepted and included like I was being now, at that moment.

And then I heard the faint sound of a familiar song that someone I love used to play for me on Friday nights. Was it? No, it couldn't be.

I googled the song. Yes! It was Daft Punk and it was a song from the only album Pack bought while we were together.

Then I knew I was not only loved, accepted and included here on earth, but the one I love in Heaven was sharing the moment and telling me he loved me too.

A couple of weeks later, CP bought a car. The day after, he asked me if I wanted to go wash cars together. I remembered that special day I had experienced with Pack and I remembered Pack's joy, so I said yes. It was a full circle moment. It felt amazing to finally be in this moment again, especially with the man whose friendship has most healed my grief.

Then I got in my car and there was a single white feather on the driver's seat that wasn't there when I got out of it. So I guess Pack and I did get to wash our cars together again after all.

Cherry Pie

I learned how to bake a cherry pie on Christmas Day.

I was forty-one then. It was long before my melee with Daniel, my growth with Reginald, and my solid foundation with God. I really didn't know how to do adult things like that then, but I had to. So God stepped in and helped me. I didn't even have to ask. That's the thing about God, He always shows up on time. And with God, you're never alone.

What happened was, my father really wanted a cherry pie for Christmas and he mistakenly bought one you had to bake. Due to his Parkinson's, he doesn't have the cognitive skills to think everything through now. My mother tried to do it, but she couldn't because she got confused. That's what happens now though. She doesn't know how to do most things that people do anymore. She's not stupid either, though. She's a beautiful child of God.

As the pie was baking, my mother broke down. Through sobs, she said words I had known were coming for a couple of years but that had, until that moment, been brutally fought away.

"I'm confused a lot and I'm scared and I feel like I'm dying."

"I know," I replied. "It's time to get you some help. You don't have to hurt this much. Will you let me help you?"

I know that last part wasn't me because I was terrified. I'm a middle-aged gay man. I've never had children. I do not want children. I only started taking care of myself in sobriety, and I only got good at that when I started humbling myself by getting on my knees and asking God for His help. We were not there yet. Or

The Sparkle King

so I thought.

And as we both cried hard, after years of fighting, she finally accepted my help. It was sad and scary and awful, but it was also the most humbling and beautiful thing I've ever witnessed. I have helped her ever since then. We went from being unable to be in the same room together when I was being a selfish idiot at the height of my drug addiction, to me standing up for her in doctors' offices and being her voice. I need to do that, as she doesn't have one of her own anymore.

Almost a year and a half prior to this huge moment, I had tried to jump out of a 26th story window in Las Vegas and my mother had somehow—this I know was God—saved me by finding me before I did it. On that night, a paramedic had spelled all of this out for me. The way the light hit her from the back, she looked like an angel. I was too wasted from four days of excessive meth use and drinking to realize she was actually preparing me for my future. The whole thing was a prophecy—God was getting me ready. Thank God I was smart enough to admit my powerlessness that night, so I could step into my power and be the man she—and my father-by-proxy—needed me to be.

As I wailed and sobbed and prepared to be taken away to the hospital, I basically told her I was scared to take care of my parents without the help of my dead partner—who had really taken care of me, if I'm being honest.

"How can you take care of anyone else if you can't take care of yourself?" the paramedic asked. And then my miracle began—I got sober in that hospital, I worked the steps, I began helping others. All these things happened in perfect succession and were perfectly timed by God, so that his perfect plan could manifest for me. I didn't know it then, but with every new challenge, He was forcing me to man up, preparing me for battle. And even though taking care of two elderly, dying parents isn't my will, it is God's. How dare I not step up to the plate and do the work He decided I was ready for?

I'm even grateful for this task. It's forced me to grow up—and man up—in ways I didn't realize. I've learned the value of patience. I've definitely learned the power and necessity of prayer. And even though I feel terrified and frightened that my parents are dying right before my eyes, I also feel great hope because this daunting task is forcing me to look to God, which in turn forces me to become the capable man I really am. With God on my side, I can do anything. So now I do.

Hope is an experience in life that leads us to a greater awakening. It acknowledges that we are hurting, struggling, feeling helpless or going through a hard time. Hope is part of our nature, our soul, our spirit. It actually lets us feel our pain so that it can lead us to an ultimate breakthrough. Because when we awaken to the hope that God's Love provides, we intuitively know something better is on the horizon. We follow the whisper and let hope—and God—make magic together so that we can manifest miracles. This is what life is like in the flow.

As God does His work, He uses this hope to open a pathway to our dreams. You don't need to know how He does it. Just hold the vision and prepare for the magic—His magic.

The rainbow in this cloud is that God is here. He has shown up for me and taught me how to man-up, so that I can show up for my parents. That means if I need to figure out how to bake a cherry pie on the fly, I will intuitively know how to solve problems that used to baffle me.

God is a magician and through his love, guidance and grace, I can do anything. I feel grateful I get to do things for her now. And yes, I said *get*. Anything I get to do for the woman who gave me life twice is a privilege and an honor. So, whether it's making a cherry pie or climbing through a dumpster to look for the new earrings she's lost, or having the same conversation every time I see her, I'm going to figure out how to do it. Because I get to be the man my parents need today.

The Sparkle King

Home

I had just worked my first week at an all-men's rehab center, which consisted of four, twelve-hour shifts that went through the night. I was exhausted and delirious from tricking my body into being awake when it usually slept, and vice versa.

I knew my mother had a lunchtime doctor's appointment that she needed me to help her with, but I was really tired. I needed to sleep beforehand to be of any real use to her.

I thought that if I went to my apartment I'd never get up in time. I knew that if I went home—a place full of warmth, peace and happy memories—I'd feel so much safety and love that I would sleep like a baby.

I drove from work to my parents' new condo. They had moved from my boyhood home a few blocks away a few years prior, but since then I had still found refuge when I was sick. It doesn't matter where "home" was, I learned, it's about the people in it.

On this day, the lights were on but nobody was home.

Maybe it was sheer exhaustion, or maybe it was the dramatic wake-up call I had been avoiding for a solid year or so. But I knew when I got there, my parents' illnesses had turned the corner from bad to worse. And they weren't coming back from this one.

The first thing I noticed was the stench of urine. This probably wasn't that surprising—my mother had begged for more time with my dogs because she said they made her feel like she had something to live for. As such, I had agreed to let her take them for weeks at a time. Both are potty-trained in theory. While I know they know better, Miley likes to mark his territory and Chloe likes to mark her man's.

But then I turned the corner and saw large piles of trash on the kitchen sink and in the living room. I saw poop lying in the middle of the floor in my dad's bedroom. I pulled out a dish from the pantry to have some cereal and it was dirty. I pulled out another. Dirty. And another. Dirty. Then I peered in my mother's room. Not only was the trash mounting, everything was dirty. There were dirty clothes. On. The. Floor. Then I saw a row of half-drank cola cans next to my mother's bed and knew it was a sign of the Armageddon.

The sheer alternate reality of this world I had entered was jarring. I felt like screaming "No More cola" at the top of my lungs, à la Joan Crawford when she demanded, "NO MORE WIRE HANGERS" in *Mommie Dearest.* After all, this was my mother's house I was in. This was a woman who had spent her life following me around and cleaning up after me. And everyone else who came into her ornately decorated, over-the-top in color, slightly wacky-style golf course home for that matter. She was like a human vacuum cleaner.

But she wasn't any of those things anymore. I didn't recognize this person.

My mother has shown signs of dementia for about five years and more recently, she has slipped even more. About six months ago, she wrote a $3,000 check and put it in the church offertory – I had to hunt it down and rip up. She also lost her driver's license recently when she got in to her sixth small car accident and could not tell the police what had happened. But this one felt different—she was Thelma and had full-on driven off a cliff without Louise. And it was the saddest fucking thing I ever saw in my whole life.

I locked myself in my dad's room. I tried to meditate. But all I could do was sob. I lay there in his bed—he was completely oblivious, like always, just one room away—and felt the sadness of this grim discovery. I wailed and sobbed and silently screamed as I felt the whole thing in its gross and totally disarming totality. It was emotionally torturous but I knew from experience that I had to heal it to feel it. So I did.

Let me make it clear: crying is not a sign of weakness; it's a sign of strength. So is reaching out and asking for help, which I did on Facebook. My army of beautiful friends rallied behind me and mostly gave me great advice, as well as a lot of love. It was enough to get me ready for the next battle at the doctor's office.

Lately, my mother sleeps for about twenty hours a day. She doesn't seem depressed—actually, whatever this disease is that takes parts of her away from me every time I see her, it has made her very pleasant and loving, which proves I'm no longer dealing with my mother. I'm not going to complain. I will take it. My dad is always short—and sometimes very cutting and cruel—so one easy patient out of two is a welcome reprieve.

On this day, when I looked at her, there was more going on with her than the vacant abyss of nothingness that now greets me in her dead-looking eyes. Something was very off, but I couldn't put my finger on it. Her skin, leathery and coarse from years of sun and smoking, looked rougher, different than usual. She was laying down in bed—in complete silence, which is her new norm—and everything about it just looked *uncomfortable*. I asked her if she was alright. She said yes—she always says yes now—and then she stood up.

A petite woman—at 5'1" she might weigh 105 pounds on a good day—my mother was even less than she had ever been. Her clothes hung off her bony frame. Even worse, her ragged, aged skin hung on her tiny body. She lunged toward me like something out of a horror movie. It was as if the Crypt Keeper had swallowed my mother and was coming after me for a feeding. Or she was auditioning for *Thriller*. I wasn't sure.

I swallowed my fear and did what I do best: I just loved her. I told her she was beautiful, and that she was brave and amazing and wonderful, and that we were

The Sparkle King

going to have a very special day together. Yes, even in the most hopeless situation, The Sparkle King can 'turn up the joy.' That's why everyone likes me now.

We got to the doctor's office. This particular doctor—a man my mother used to work with when she took care of people just like her, with dementia—is always an hour late. By this point, sheer fatigue was adding to the desperate brokenness I felt in my heart.

Over the past year, I've had to become her voice for her at these appointments. According to her, everything is "fine"—she even smiles when she says it. But I think that comes from years of telling everyone that everything is fine when it isn't—she grew up with an abusive father who tortured her emotionally and a distant mother who tried to love her but was stopped by her father. In fact, my grandfather cut my grandmother's head off in every picture she was in and called her "The Thing."

Then my mother married my father and they fought and hated each other, putting me in the middle of it all. However, they were both too weak—too codependent—to do the right thing and divorce. I frankly don't blame her brain for taking a vacation from her body. She has to be exhausted.

We started with the normal "I feel fine" banter on this day. Normally, I always jump in and say what's really going on: "We had to take the checkbook away," "She got in another car accident," "She's sleeping twenty hours a day". This time, however, I just started sobbing. The doctor—who knew my mother at her heady heyday of colorful behavior and delirious grandiosity—consoled me:

"You're being a very good son. It's obvious you love your mother very much."

And it's true. She was completely batshit crazy most of my life and she was such an evil nightmare when I grieved my dead lover—I even tried to jump out of a twenty-six-story window in a casino in Las Vegas to evade her. But she was also the woman who had given me life twice: first when she gave birth to me and then later, when she called my bluff on that tortured, scary last evening of methamphetamine and alcohol use. In doing so, she saved me from myself once and for all. Plus, if we are being honest, everything I don't like about her is what I don't like about myself. I'm just as colorful, off-kilter and broken—I just know how to lean in to my pain and make it power. I've turned it in to an art.

As I cried, my mother stood up and weighed herself. The doctor noted she had lost fifteen pounds in just a month. Now he was concerned. He ordered blood work, which meant it would now be even longer before I finally would sleep. I was actually somewhat grateful I was half-crazed on this day, because I think I needed to be in order to move past complacency and into action. I made a silent vow on that day to start doing what I needed to do to get my parents in to care. A tough, long road awaits me.

My mother was actually hungry by the time we were done at the doctor, so we grabbed lunch. I take her to church every Sunday. We always have lunch after. She barely speaks during these meals, and while my head is full of fear and worst case scenarios that play out dramatically while we sit together, I am always able to pull it together and stay in the moment with her. This is a gift of daily meditation. This day was no different than all the others. I looked across from her and smiled at her. She smiled back. It's a far cry from the torture and worry I put her through when I was using. This is God's Plan—a beautiful way to help me make amends and I am lucky to get the chance to do so. I will do whatever I have to do to make her feel safe and sound—and loved.

It is a gift from God we have this easy, loving relationship now. It should be noted that less than three years ago, I couldn't be in the same room with her without having to be high. Now there is nowhere I would rather be and no one I would rather be there for.

I asked my mother how she was coping with not driving.

"I hate it," she said. "I don't feel like a person anymore."

I redirected: "Lots of people don't drive!"

"Like who?" she asked, rolling her eyes.

"Mature women with memory issues," I said.

She shot me a glare. "MATURE?!?"

"Yes, mature," I said. "You're lucky I didn't call you old. I was being nice."

And then she tilted her head back and started laughing hysterically. I hadn't seen her laugh that way—with so much joy and happiness—since this whole Alzheimer's debacle started, so I laughed too.

Dance With My Father

Long-term sobriety means that you have to man up and do a lot of stuff that you really don't want to do.

I have a sponsor that cuts to the core of my bullshit and challenges me to be more than I ever thought I could be. Which can only mean he is a true vessel of the Divine, because when I pray, I don't ask for more—I ask to become more.

Recently, I've pushed myself in surprising ways that have been crucial for my growth into emotional sobriety. I helped my friends build a house for a needy family in Mexico. I quit a safe job I had been in for seven years because I heard a whisper telling me that if I chose faith over fear, I'd be rewarded. I didn't retaliate when a publicist stole several thousand dollars from me; I prayed for him. I've stepped up to be my mother's primary caregiver; I'm about to do the same for my father. I kicked a man out of my house when he disrespected me in my own home. I didn't fall apart when Daniel denounced me; I got closer to God. I say "No" when I don't want to do something. I even went camping. It turns out my prayers are being answered because I am nowhere near the person I used to be. I'm a man now.

So, when my sponsor Reginald asks me to do something—I do it. History tells me there is a reason he is asking me to do something. The direct result of my actions is a new level of freedom and completeness that I have never before imagined.

Reginald tested me though, recently, when he asked me to properly make amends with my father.

"I've already made amends with my father," I said incredulously. "I apologized for being high at his birthday party and for not being around when I was using."

"That's not a real amends," my sponsor shot back.

And he was right. Those type of 'amends' work for friends and some family members. But when you have the type of tortured, broken relationship I've shared with my father, there are a lot of nuances—little hurts that add up to big emotional whammy's over time—that need to be evaluated.

The truth is, my father has Parkinson's and is just as sick, if not worse, than my mother. But I totally caretake to my mother and mostly ignore my father. Sure, I took him on a couple of trips back home to Iowa when we were getting along better a few years ago, but for whatever reason, our relationship had deteriorated greatly since then and I had been unwilling to look at why.

Out of nowhere, my father would totally snap at me—and utterly destroy me—with a few cutting words. Then I would scream and cry at him. Then he'd be meaner. Then I would storm out and tell him I'd never speak to him again. And then I'd call or go back a couple of hours later and make my daily "amends."

It was time to nip this emotional terrorism in the bud. My sponsor suggested that maybe psychologically I was still punishing him for being a shitty father and making me feel abandoned as a child.

"But he's the one randomly throwing a fit about nothing," I countered. "He just goes off for no reason."

But then I thought about what my sponsor had said and I realized that he was right. Since both of my parents have been sick I have doted on, and even spoiled, my mother. I race to her side two, or sometimes three times a week. We go to meals together, to church, to movies. I rarely ask my father if he needs anything. I can't remember the last time we did something together. He's not a talker—he's a stuffer prone to immediate and almost violent outbursts of rage. So I tend to just let him do his thing and watch TV. But as I thought about it, I realized I was nowhere near there for him in the way I was for my mother. So it suddenly made sense that he raged at me the way he did. He was a human being—a very sick, elderly human being—who was watching his partner of forty-seven years deteriorate right in front of his eyes. Oh, by the way, every step he takes is riddled with pain because his nerves cry out in torture every time he steps on them.

"So when are you going to apologize to your father?" my sponsor asked.

"Oh, tomorrow will be fine. I was just there."

"You're going right now," he shot back.

So I did. I drove straight to see my father, who was in exactly the same place he was when I was there earlier in the day—in front of the TV, glued to it as always.

I told him I needed to talk to him. I hoped he would turn off the TV so we could talk. He turned it down, which is about as much as he could handle. Since this was about meeting him where he was at, I pressed on. I told him I had been thinking.

And then forty-three years of pain left my body. I leveled with him. I simply told him the truth:

"Psychologically, I am a five-year-old boy who feels unloved by you and now I'm the adult and you are the child, so I am unconsciously punishing you."

"Children should be seen but not heard."—Those were his own words toward me throughout my whole childhood. Only now, the tables were turned. Whew—a huge weight lifted—a breakthrough—a full circle 'aha' moment!

"I know," he said. "And I'm starting to hate the sight of you."

His words stung. And then he said a lot of other things I didn't want to hear. But for about an hour, I just shut up and listened to him. And then I realized he needed help too. He was a broken man with a heartbreaking degenerative disease, caught in an even more heartbreaking situation that was unfolding around him as parts of his wife disappeared every day, courtesy

The Sparkle King

of dementia. He couldn't take care of himself and he couldn't take care of her and they couldn't take care of each other. This was the end of the road for them.

There I was, working through tough stuff with my most unlikely client of all time: my father. I could tell he enjoyed the audience. His posture was better and he even smiled—even though half the stuff he said was totally crazy. I noticed that his once sharp, too-intelligent-for-his-own-good personality had shifted to one that all too often seemed confused and unable to reason normally. But the important thing was that I was open and I was present in that moment; a gift of meditation and from God. It cemented what I knew needed to happen more than ever: I needed to get both of them more help.

Though I felt better having this very human and cathartic moment with my father, I left my meeting with him feeling a lot of fear. The road to getting them the help they needed was going to be rough and I knew it. And, as an only child, I was completely alone in it.

Well, not completely alone. I woke up the next morning feeling so depleted. Between the drama that week with my mother and that emotionally exhausting amends with my father, I just felt done.

Though it was Easter, I didn't want to go to church or deal with my parents or really deal with anyone. I felt angry that all of this was happening. I felt alone and hopeless, so I asked God why I was alone and hopeless. Why was all this happening? Why did all this tough stuff always happen to me? Why couldn't I ever just know peace?

Then I saw a mysterious link in a blank text message on my phone. It didn't say who it was from or what it was, but I clicked on it because my whisper told me to take it seriously. It was a beautiful devotional, reminding me that even though I might not be where I want to be, I needed to remember how far I had come.

I thanked the mystery sender in prayer.

Then the phone rang. It was Rosie, one of my friends

from my recent peer support class. I had not talked to her or seen her since class but Rosie—a deeply spiritual black woman who radiated God's grace from her pores—said God put it on her heart to send me the devotional because she could feel my pain from where she was.

We talked for a while and she said that God wanted me to know that this all wasn't happening to me, it was happening FOR me, as He knew how strong I was.

"Count it all as joy," she said. "For the testing of your faith is building you up."

This short and loving exchange was exactly what I needed to rebuild my fire again. And it was especially spectacular because it was proof that God heard my prayers. After all, I had just called out to Him in pain. And He answered me like he always does, reminding me to keep choosing faith over fear—and moving me to change into the man He wanted me to become. Because I had asked Him to help me do this, many times prior.

The Sparkle King

I Was Here

The night before I found my partner dead, he went to bed early because he didn't feel well.

About half an hour after he went into his room, he texted me: "Can you please come in here right now?"

I walked into his room.

"Will you please come in here and lie next to me?" he asked. "I'm scared."

And so I honored his last wish. For about twenty minutes, until he felt safe enough to fall asleep, we laid there. I felt his love for the last time and he felt mine for the last time.

I was there.

This experience taught me the most valuable lesson I have ever learned: the most important thing you can ever do for someone you love is to be there for them. That's it: just show up. Whether you want to or not, just being there for the people you love is just about all that matters.

My partner and I were only together for three years. When I was grieving, I used to wonder if I would have stayed, had I known the outcome prior to engaging in this too-short relationship.

I was given the opportunity to test my theory when I had about a year of sobriety. One of my new friends, a charismatic and wise man named Mike, had been diagnosed with cancer.

I knew he was going to die.

I was faced with a decision. Would I back away and dip out or would I stay and show up for this man I loved?

I surprised myself and stayed. I again found myself in a position to honor a dying man's wishes when Mike asked me to go to Wal-Mart and buy him some clothes to wear in the hospital. Here I was, a person once completely undone by grief, who was able to stay and be there for someone I really loved.

I was there.

Now it's a whole other year later. I find myself the only child of two parents who are both facing significant health issues. My father has had Parkinson's for several years, and my mom is starting to dive deep into Alzheimer's. The rapid pace at which she is slipping is scary. Sometimes she doesn't even know what day it is.

But these experiences have taught me that as long as I am there—as long as I am present—we can get through this. Plus I'm sober now. And if I've learned anything in recovery, I can do just about anything sober. Because I am able to be present in a way I wasn't before.

Recently, I accompanied my mom to church. I happened to notice the check she put in the offertory was for $3,000. I knew that she didn't mean to make it for that much money. I was able to talk to the office and stop them from cashing it. My father looked at me like a hero. My mom still has no idea I did that, but I was already her hero that day.

Because I was there.

And I always will be. Because love is all there is. So if you are lucky enough to have it, take my advice: be present for it. Bask in the awareness and beauty of this moment. You'll be glad you were there, too.

My mom only recently became willing to see a doctor that is a memory specialist. We've been winging it for this whole time, but her memory issues have become dire. When we got to his office, there had been a mix-up with her insurance paperwork. They could not see her that day, they said. We had waited several months for this appointment.

I knew we didn't have more time to wait to get her help, so I refused to leave.

"Do you see that beautiful woman over there?" I

asked.

"Yes," she said.

"That woman is my mother and we have been waiting for this appointment for months. She is scared because this is a life or death issue for her and you WILL see her TODAY because I love her too much to let this happen to her."

Her eyes softened and she looked at the other receptionist. She nervously shuffled papers around and asked me to sit down. "Let me see what I can do," she said.

About five minutes later my prayers were answered when without explanation, we were invited to the back of the office. "The doctor will see you now."

When the receptionist weighed my mom, I noticed she was wearing sparkly shoes. I took it as a sign that Pack was there with me; that we were in the right place. And because I was willing to get loud for love, I got to be there yet again for the woman who gave me life twice.

The Sparkle King

Hold Up the Light

I don't know if the glass is half full or half empty, but I do know that if you have something to drink, you should thank God for it.

I also don't know if a tree makes a sound when it falls in the woods, but I do know you should thank God for it, because nature is beautiful.

I may never know why my life was filled with so much darkness and pain for so long, but I do know I am now actually thankful to God for all of it. How could I be anything but grateful for the series of terrible, no-good events that forced me to move out of my pain and into the mighty power I reside in today? I sparkle as bright as I can, so that I can share my light with others who still may be coming out of the dark.

This never-ending flow of gratitude that lives and breathes in me has turned on a light inside my soul that has opened the path to let grace flow through me. I now know that if I want to manifest blessings, I need to start by getting very serious about what I am already grateful for.

So let me make it clear right here, right now. I want to give all my haters a standing ovation for helping me figure out who I really am. It is actually all of you that birthed my sparkle. It is because of you I love myself enough to shine as bright as I do. It is also because of you that I vow to spend the rest of my life using my sparkle to fight hate and fear with love and light.

To the boys who threw rocks at me in Kindergarten, rendering me afraid to go to school: thank you for your part in making me strong. You can throw whatever you want at me now, as I picked faith over the fear you caused and the God I found in doing so won't let you hurt me ever again.

To the kids who made fun of me in the third grade when I wore that red and black jacket that was similar to the one Michael Jackson wore for *Thriller*: you inspire me to proudly sashay across every threshold I arrive at in my beautiful sparkly shoes.

To the boys in the sixth grade who tricked me into eating a Ding Dong that was laced with a laxative: thank you for giving me the gift of discernment that I have honed in on as my whisper. I'm able to follow my intuition today, so that I don't have to worry about betrayal like that anymore.

To the boys in high school who tried to drown me at every pool party, who teased me so mercilessly that I became known as *The Whipping Boy*. You can't hurt me anymore. Thank you for letting me experience hate so that I would know the opposite: a real, true, Divine love that only God can give me. And by the way, I'm the Sparkle King now, so your cruel nickname holds no weight anymore.

To the guys who attacked me in a hallway in college and forced me to the ground, where you held me against my will and beat my face with phallic socks: Thank you for helping me realize I was gay so I could come out and be fabulous. So many people never do so because they are afraid. Like my dead partner Pack, they never stand in their truth. Because of you, I do, and I am proud of who I am.

To the man I loved who beat me, kicked me, spat on me and screamed at me, yelling names like "faggot," "nigger," and "whore." Insults that still ring in my ears every day. Thank you for delivering me to Pack with your abuse. It is through him I experienced the greatest, easiest, most accessible love I have ever experienced with a man. I never would have found him without you.

To Pack's family, who threw me out of our home, ransacked it and left it a mess, then forbade me to attend his funeral: your hate made me stronger than I have ever been in my whole life. You caused the greatest pain I've ever felt. Because of that, I have harnessed this pain into a mighty power that is full of love and that has propelled me to places I never imagined. There would be no sparkle without you. Perhaps I owe you the most gratitude of all. I bow to you.

To the drugs and addiction that almost caused me to fly out of a Vegas casino window: thank you for making me a mess so that I could hit rock bottom and become sober. It is in this amazing space of recovery that I gave birth to the force I am: a man who can do anything he sets his mind on. It is in the darkness we spent together on the floor of my closet that I transformed from a dingy lump of coal into the glorious, dazzling, radiant, light-shifting diamond of a man that I am today.

To all the people who judge me for living with bipolar: you inspire me to fight for myself and people like me. Your judgement moves me to stand in my truth and be a voice for the voiceless, as they are still afraid to be themselves because you've abused them with your hate. I will continue to shout our abilities from the rafters. I'm not afraid to be who I am because God made me this way, and I know the God I love does not make mistakes.

To all of you, any source of hurt in my entire life: I thank you over and over and over again. You helped me find my light. I'm going to hang out here in it and toast you all for showing me who you really are. They say when someone shows you who they really are, you should believe them the first time. I see only the truth now: that all your abuse created a beautiful, marvelous, glorious, resilient, powerful child of God who is able to love you in spite of all you did. This is because the happiness I now know comes from within and is not from anything external. I know I have no control over any of your behavior. I also know that makes me more powerful than you ever thought I could be.

I am in awe of all that pain I just described because without it, I would have never have become attuned to who I really am. And I like this guy. The man I am is a winner—a man full of love and light. Light that I first give to myself so that I may let it multiply and shine on the rest of the world. For I know that it is only in loving myself in the beautiful and real way that I do, that I can stand before the world and be the glittery powerhouse that I am now.

This space of gratitude in which I live today is like a secret key that has shifted my awareness and perception. In this space of light, I accept and appreciate all of these things instead of questioning and rejecting them.

It is in doing all of this that I unlock the power that creates new opportunities for grace and light to enter my life. And my future looks so bright, I'm almost blinded by it.

There For Me

It would take all of my life to find someone more there for me than my oldest friend, Melissa.

She is also a drug addict, which means she has spent her own time in the dark—and some of it was so bad that we parted for a while due to some awful things I said to retaliate against her for "wrongs" I felt she had dealt me. However, God saw to it to bring us back together in sobriety.

I've actually always thought it funny that we weren't friends while I was in my soul-engulfing relationship with Pack. It's almost as if she let go of me just at the right time so that I could go to him, allowing me to give him the love he needed to complete his life so that he could die. That's how big our love is—it's the kind of grace that fuels your soul and makes you believe love is bigger and lasts longer than everything and anything that tries to get in its way.

I've known Melissa twenty-two years. Yes, our friendship is a full-on adult one, and even though we are both in our forties now—me early, her super late—we are as fun, whimsical, magical and wonderful as we were nearly fifteen years ago, when we cemented our relationship by deciding we were forever to be Birkie Boy and Birkie Girl.

Since everyone always asks: legend has it that Melissa, then a new mother, went shopping with her baby, my mother and I. I had seen a pair of Birkenstocks that I wanted, but my mother would not buy them for me. This was odd, as my mother still spoiled me back then, to the point that I was like a baby.

Later that evening, my mother called Melissa and left

a super-sloppy, yet totally hilarious drunken message on her answering machine—yes, that's how long ago this was. She was delightfully slurring every word and promising that as I had "been such a good boy that day," she was going to buy me Birkies after all! The whole thing was so absurd because I was in my mid-twenties and I was being rewarded for being a 'good boy' while we actually shopped with an infant. I remember we played the message over and over again, and I know we laughed harder and fell to the ground in near tears every time we did.

It's memories like that which comprise the foundation of our now unshakable bond. From day one, we've been a team. There were very early memories, where I was still too scared to be gay – but still so gay that I invited her and our co-worker Georgann over to my house to have a "Cinderella" party. This was to celebrate Whitney Houston's new TV movie.

Then there was the time when I was in trouble with our boss and he wouldn't let me 'go to her', despite the fact I was crying in front of the whole newsroom. There was even the time when she copy-edited one of my early stories and failed to see the word *whore*, which meant a sentence read: *"Due to the number of whorehouses in Tolleson, the population doubles during the day."* That one made it all the way to Jay Leno.

There was also the first time I met her former husband, Jason. The three of us went to a Rolling Stones concert and I interrupted it with almost delirious screaming, yelling out "Oh my god, it's Lisa Fischer!" when I realized their background singer was my favorite nineties R&B chanteuse.

There was also the time when I first saw her child in her belly, on the day of her first doctor's appointment. I was the first person to see the image and it was just a dot on a screen. It was on that same day that we stopped to get ice cream and she ordered a weird flavor. At the time, I shouted "My God, you're a nasty pregnant woman" so loudly that everyone in the shop could hear me.

I was also there when that baby was just a year old and we bought gold lame fabric and dressed him up like an Oscar for the Oscars that year. There was also the fact that she taught that boy, Casper, and her daughter, Noe, to call me Uncle Patrick.

When I moved away for five years in my late twenties, she and Jason and those kids were so my chosen family that whenever I came to visit, I stayed with them. Hence why my mother had to leave a voice message about Birkies in the first place. However, it's the difficult part in the middle, between this early joy and the easy-going place of love and lifetime camaraderie we reside in today, where we had to take a break. By doing this though, we could come back together, stronger than ever. What I know for sure is that I have never had a friend like my Birkie Girl.

We were apart for a full five years. In that time I loved—and lost—Pack. I also became a raging drug addict. And maybe because she is one too, she was able to offer me the grace and forgiveness I didn't deserve when mutual sobriety brought us back together again. Even though all that time had passed—and so much had happened to both of us—we picked up right where we left off. We are so close, I believe she knows Pack in her soul even though they never met. Maybe she is able to do this because the two of them comprise one half of my now fully beating, thriving heart.

I also know she always feels like I choose everyone else—especially men—over her. But I want my oldest adult friend—the one who cares enough to bring me soup and medicine when I am sick; the one who shows up to every stupid little thing I do and cheers for me; the one who chooses me no matter what; the one who has rushed forward to help me deal with my parents and their illnesses when family members have abandoned me; the one who is honest and loves me enough to tell me truths I don't want to hear; the one who protects me from my ridiculous flights of whimsy by always looking out for me; the one who puts up with my crazy rants and my near-stalker behavior with men like Daniel and never judges me; the one I have this shared history with; and perhaps especially, the one who resides in my living, beating heart and whose love I feel more than any other—to know that I see you, I appreciate you, and I love you the most, too.

Moment of Truth

When someone shows you who they are, it's best to believe them the first time.

I had just started working for 'friends' at a new rehab center for men. While I loved the work—I was especially excited about the narrative of how a gay man who was once bullied by men became a leader of them—I could never shake the whisper that my boss didn't have my best interests at heart.

Things kept happening that showed me who he really was, but I desperately wanted it to work. Life and God, however, have a way of making you face situations repeatedly until you conquer them the way you are supposed to.

I knew that it was a new venture and I also knew that when you start out in the recovery world, you have to start at the bottom and work your way up. As such, I was not surprised when my start date got pushed up a week. I dropped everything—including birthday plans—to show up and be there with just a few hours' notice.

It was obvious from the jump that many things at this new place were being decided on the fly, but one thing that seemed hopeful was that since it was new, I felt like there was an opportunity to make it my own and put my stamp on things.

That was until I actually started working there.

The very first day I had not brought dinner—I didn't know what to expect—so my new boss took me to get some fast food. I knew him casually and socially, but Mark and I were not particularly close. He had always been friendly to me, so I had no problem with him. But as we were going through the drive-thru, they got our order wrong. Mark went nuclear on them. He was rude, insulting:

"How could anyone be so stupid?" he bellowed.

In his overreaction, I caught my first glimpse of what life was going to be like if I ever crossed him. As scary as that vision was, I'm still glad I eventually did, because I show up for and honor myself today.

As I started the actual work, I fell in love with it. I loved the instant connection I had with those broken men. I loved sharing myself with them and listening as they shared themselves with me. I loved being there for them; being able to help another person work through difficult life events because I already had. It was beautiful and human and real and true. I was so excited to be sharing this work experience with people who needed me. It was a blessing.

But it was also challenging for me. I had never worked in this field before—and I was working completely by myself, at night, with zero supervision—so I did stumble a bit, mostly around rules. These kept changing anyway, by the way. I kept being told that it was okay to ask questions but then when I did, I was either ignored or made to feel like those poor fast food workers. There were also conditions that really don't seem feasible for a business in operation. For instance, the night we moved into our house there was no running water, which meant that employees and residents who were spending thousands of dollars for rehab couldn't go to the bathroom. But I chalked it up to things being new and let it go. These 'pebbles' were not deal breakers for me.

Another problem I was having was the hours. The shifts were twelve-hours long and I had three shifts one week and four the next. This seemed like a smoking deal because it meant I had four days off every two weeks. However, working twelve-hour shifts through the middle of the night was not only physically demanding, it was psychologically demanding too. Also—another pebble, perhaps—there were no benefits to start.

'Maybe there will be in the future,' I thought to myself.

That alone should have been a deal breaker in retrospect. That shows a general lack of respect or care for people.

Then Mark threw the rock. When I got hired, he had promised me I would be the first person moved to day shift. But then I was not the first person moved there. Or the second. Or the third. And I think he thought that he could get away with lying to me, but I don't live like that way in sobriety: I stand up for myself. Plus, even though I do tend to waver when actual conflict is involved, when I told Reginald about it, he asked me to address it with Mark. And we have already established that Reginald doesn't really ask for things. So the next time there was an issue, I confronted him.

This moment occurred fairly soon after my discussion with Reginald.

Mark had sent a typically antagonistic text: "Why haven't you called me today?"

"Because I just woke up and you did not leave me a message to do so," I replied.

"Well, from now on, when I call, that means I want you to call me back."

My inner bitch responded: *'Yes sir, I'll do better at mindreading from now on.'* The actual man I am replied: "Okay, there are some miscommunication issues happening overall. I am in fear about communicating them, but my sponsor told me I need to say something."

So I called him. I confronted him about the issue of not being moved to a better shift first, as promised. His response was another lie:

"There have been ... performance ... issues."

But there had not been. Or at least, I had never been apprised of them. In fact, in the two staff meetings we'd had, I had received the most praise for my work, which might have been his guilt-assuaging him for promoting other less-qualified people.

"I need to ... I need to call you right back," he said, before hanging up.

I think he must have needed to call the owner or someone else to help him concoct the 'truth.' He called back, sticking to the performance issue excuse. So I leaned in:

"Was I ever going to be told you had issues with me or was I going to keep stumbling around the dark?" It should be noted that I met this man in a men's accountability meeting. But there would be none of this day. He didn't really answer the question. He made up some excuse about having a family dinner.

"We can talk more later," he said. "My door is open."

But we didn't and it wasn't. The next time I heard from Mark, it was another text, on my day off: "Hey Patrick, can you come by the office around 4 p.m. today?"

The writing was on the wall. Bosses don't call employees in on their day off at 4 p.m. on a Friday to tell them they are doing a good job. There's also the part where people being dishonest don't like being held accountable for their actions.

I immediately felt panic. I have intense fear around being fired. I had once been the managing editor of the largest gay magazine in the Southwest. I got fired from it in the midst of being abused by the man I was in a relationship with and turned to drugs as a result. Being fired is actually my greatest fear—and here it was, happening again.

As my 4 p.m. tête-a-tête with Mark loomed, I got busy doing what I do now when I am in fear—I prayed and meditated. I asked God for strength and I asked my angels to protect me.

I still had to take my mom to get her hair done on that day. She sat in silence and stared ahead of her like a lifeless zombie as we headed there, but for some reason, I started telling her what was going on. I shared how much fear I was experiencing, and how I truly felt about this job, and what I heard in the echo of her silence astounded me. I heard myself saying that if I got fired they were doing me a favor because I did not want to work for people who didn't treat me right. I heard myself say I wanted out. I heard myself say I deserved better. Yes, the boy who used to be afraid was no longer afraid. I am not that boy anymore. I am a man who stands up and fights for myself—and others like me.

My mom leaned over and touched me, saying nothing. In her touch, I again felt everything I had just 'heard.' Her silence had, in fact, allowed me to answer myself. Her silence had allowed me to hear my whisper, and this time I knew that even if I wasn't fired, I had to quit. Either way, I was setting myself free.

After this moment of realization in the silence of my mother's quiet but potent response, I immediately found a feather. Then, when I wasn't touching it, my phone started playing *'Life's About to Get Good,'* by Shania Twain.

After I dropped my mother off, I drove toward the dreaded meeting. On the way, the song *'Moment of Truth'* by Whitney Houston kept repeating when I didn't ask it to. I thanked my dead lover for his sense of humor.

So I went there at 4 p.m. to face the music. I could feel the fear bubbling up inside me, telling me to run, but I could feel even greater faith calming me down and reassuring me it was all going to be okay if I faced this.

And then I got fired. I did not cry. I did not sob. I did not wail. I did not overreact. I did not scream. I did not argue. I did not call anyone names. I did not blame. I did not make excuses.

I just looked at Mark in the power I was creating out of this very painful moment and said, "Thank you."

Then he said a bunch of nice, placating stuff like "I hope we can still be friends."

And why not? Though I am not going to race over to be his bestie, I will still be friendly toward him. I will especially pray for him. Because this is what I know about grace: the more we offer it to people who may not deserve it—but who need it more than others—the more we multiply light and love. I am far too mature and loved by God to let the dishonest and disingenuous actions of one person stop me from shining my light for all. Yes, as Whitney sang, learning to love yourself is the greatest love of all! I may have 'failed' at this job but I really succeeded, as I learned to depend on me. They can't take away my dignity because I love, honor and know myself.

As I was getting up to leave, a guy in the room who I didn't know prior to this said to me: "Patrick, I want you to know I'm really impressed with you. You took that like a real man. I can tell you work a really good program."

"Thank you," I said. "I do, and I know God's got this."

And then I walked out of the room. I felt as though I had just conquered all of my fears and took the first step, even though I couldn't see the whole staircase. All because God told me it would be fine through my whisper, and I had enough faith to believe it to be so.

Waking Up In Vegas

The last time I got fired from a job, I set into motion a series of events that rendered me a raging crackhead.

This time, I called CP and told him I was going to pick him up. "Never mind that mine is currently in disarray, we are going to save someone else's life tonight," I said, coining a 12-Step phrase.

As I drove there, I saw several hopeful license plates that said things like *Blue Skies* and *Treasure*. Not to mention a few that spoke directly to the manifestation of my life goal to meet Oprah: *AHA*—as in moment—and *AVA*—the name of her favorite film director. It should be noted that I also keep seeing license plates that say *CAR*—Oprah is famous for giving everyone in her audience a car whilst screaming "You get a car, and you get a car, and you get a car!!" Sometimes more than one of these passes me at the same time. It's like my whisper is saying: "Oprah is going to talk to you one day." I also see the letters CBS all the time. Oprah is a correspondent for CBS now.

CP, our new friend Matt and I went to our Hospitals and Institutions meeting and lit up the room with our experience, strength and hope. I was especially on fire. I've noticed that the more pain I am in or the less I want to be somewhere, the more fired up I get. The thing is, I know what happens to me if I don't stay active and do this stuff and I've come too far to lose everything I have. I was not going to let a job that I didn't like, that I was only at for five weeks, take anything—especially my life—away from me.

Afterward, my friends took me out. Matt paid for dinner and then CP treated me to a movie. These are very simple things really, but when you are having the kind of day where you get fired just for standing in your truth, owning it, and not backing down from the fear behind it, they feel like miracles. To be so loved in this way is such a beautiful blessing. To have friends that show up for me in the way they do—it should be noted that several, including Melissa, offered to be there for me that night—is magic.

A large "Wacky Water Park" day was happening in our fellowship the next day. Reginald had asked me if I was going.

"No, I don't think it's appropriate since Daniel lives there and all," I responded.

"That wasn't a question. See you tomorrow," he huffed.

I knew I had to go and perhaps even face Daniel. It sure seemed like a lot of opportunities to face my fears were showing up for me at one time. It's a good thing I was ready to keep showing up for myself.

I woke up the next day and drove to the place where my relationship with Daniel had been a band-aid that held me in place until I found God. And again, I felt the desperate fear from my ego that nagged at me to turn around and hide out at home. And again, I told it to shut up as I faced a sure confrontation with this person who I had built up to not even be human anymore.

I should note, on the way to the event, the series of songs that played felt like a gift from my dead lover. First, I heard *'Wow'* by Kylie Minogue, which made me feel his presence. We used to mock argue with each other by rolling our eyes and shouting "*WOW*" at each other during it. Then there was *'Million Dollar Bill,'* the song that played at Christmas when I wasn't touching my phone, to remind me of my future. Then another Whitney jam, *'Step by Step,'* to keep me going. Then there was *'Money Bag'* by Cardi B., which seems self-explanatory, since I am manifesting success. And finally, *'The Climb'* by Miley Cyrus, to keep me in this moment and remind me to be grateful for all the miracles—and beauty—in it. I may not be where I want to be. But I know I am where I am supposed to be.

I've spent a lot of time at this particular halfway house. I'm also extremely well-known in our fellowship, so I can't really slink in unnoticed, never mind stay that way and be a wallflower. In fact, the moment I got there, one of my friends saw me and was so kind, so effusive, and so over-the-top with his love and respect for me, it melted away all my fear.

One by one, just about everyone who meant anything to me showed up: CP, Melissa, Reginald and Judy, a newer friend and confidant of mine who had started as a fan after she had read *Unpacked Sparkle.* She is now a lifeline and constant source of loving advice. She's also fiercely and fearlessly a champion of God and it is her faith—steadfast and resolute—that I admire most. I must also admit, it has helped me cultivate and nurture my own. I talk to her more than anyone else. She makes me see God in all of my situations, a never-ending rainbow in a burst of clouds I usually create for myself.

I had promised CP that I would help him with the 50-50 raffle. So I did. Melissa and her daughter held court, taking money for the event. Reginald seemed to be having the most fun with all the water toys and the kids. I kept finding feathers and running over to Judy and anyone else who would fancy my spiritual whimsy. Then, about one-hundred friends who were more like family splashed around, danced, laughed, lived and loved as the hot Arizona sun beat down on us and proved God was there too, smiling upon us.

I kept complaining about the music the DJ was playing. There was Rod Stewart, The Commodores, and other artists that perhaps an older crowd would enjoy. My favorite angel—DJ Pack—must have been listening all the way in Heaven, because things quickly changed and it seemed like the music was talking to me. For example, The Commodores song that played was *'Night Shift'*—an ode to the job I had just gotten fired from. Then I heard *'Right Now'* by Van Halen, which is where prayer and meditation keep me—in the moment. Then

The Sparkle King

'Waking Up in Vegas' by Katy Perry—clearly a nod to that fateful Vegas trip that caused the sobriety that would eventually bring me to this event. When I heard the beginning chords of *'I Still Haven't Found What I'm Looking For,'* I actually started to cry a little because it reminded me of CP and that beautiful, perfect camping trip a few weeks prior, where he told me I was his best friend.

I ran over to him. "They're playing our song," I said.

He perked up his ears. "Yes, they are. Bring it in, my dude." And he hugged me.

By this time I was hungry but Daniel was manning the food booth. I made tons of jokes about how I was going to ask him for his wiener—because when I am hurt or scared I always cover up with humor—but CP saw through my lame comic deflections and told me to go with him. Then CP walked over to Daniel with me and showed me what real friendship was.

He said to Daniel: "Can I have a plate for my friend?"

Again, I felt his easygoing love melting away all my fear. Now not only were men not throwing rocks at me, one was standing up for me, proving he'd make sure it never happened again. Daniel handed over a plate.

After I ate, CP and I continued to do the raffle together. At one point he said to me: "I'm glad you're doing this with me, since you know more people than I do."

I remembered how he had just helped me face my 'enemy' and I replied, "That's why we are Team CP."

As we fist-bumped, I noted how beautiful and open and present I felt in this moment, in this friendship that is the most real and true I have ever experienced. And I again exhaled. It should be noted that we raised $214 together that day, which meant $107 went to the winner. I cried a little again: Pack died on Jan. 7, or 107. The synchronicity of living in the flow was everywhere!

And then it happened. It was way later in the day and my fear had melted away. I wanted a Diet Cola and the person who had to give it to me was the one I had brought so many to when I was trying to earn his love. It was Daniel.

Suddenly I got really brave. I walked up to him and asked him if there was any cola left. And he said the first and only word he has said to me since our friendship ended.

"Diet?"

"Yes," I replied.

Both he and I knew he didn't have to ask, because he knew the answer. He knows everything about me because I shared it with him when he was my sponsor.

He handed me the drink and we made eye contact for the first time since the night he ended our relationship with that brutal, hateful phone call.

In the stillness of the moment, his eyes spoke sentences while his mouth remained closed. I saw fear. Then I saw sadness. Then without any other words exchanged between us, I felt the words I knew I would never hear from his mouth because I know he couldn't say it: His eyes told me he was sorry.

And then, just like Dorothy before me—I was even wearing a pair of red sparkly shoes that I had found whilst shopping with CP at Christmas—I peeled back the curtain and for the first time, I didn't see the deity I had made Daniel out to be. I saw a man in pain whose eyes told me he was sorry. And he was never more human to me.

As I walked away, I remembered a broken boy who stood in front of a twenty-six-story window in Las Vegas. He was so afraid of everything, he was going to jump out of it. Then I felt power surge through me, as not only was that boy gone—perhaps he did fly out that window—I was a man who faced everything he was afraid of and showed up for himself. In sobriety, I had become fearless.

As I looked around the crowd and watched my beautiful friends enjoy the day, Mike and the Mechanics' *'All I need is a Miracle'* was playing and I again realized I was living one. Because that's what you get for Waking Up in Vegas.

Turning Tables

The day after I pulled the curtain on Daniel, my mom's former Al-Anon sponsor pulled me aside at church and said there was something we needed to discuss afterward.

As she talked, the most beautiful plan—God's—that solved all my problems unspooled before me. She was going to take care of my mother in her home until we could get her into a formal care facility. This opened the door for me to move in with my father and potentially heal the only relationship in my life that has mostly been elusive to me. My father and I had experienced great times on trips to Iowa and even at the movies here or there since I got sober, but when all is said and done even when it does improve for a little while, the sticky thickness of the divide we've always shared fills in the cracks of our old fissures and keeps us apart. Billie—a recovery professional who does past life regression—put it simply: "He needs to heal his relationship with you before he can cross over."

I knew exactly what she meant. There is unfinished business between my dad and I. This forced closeness would give us the time and grace to both heal our wounds and complete him so he could move on.

My counselor in the first rehab I went to after Pack's death had said almost exactly the same thing about him: there was something about the relationship Pack had with me that had completed him and let him die. I'm going to guess it had to do with acting on his lifelong homosexuality and our mutual love—but it always made sense. Like *Jerry Maguire* said: I totally completed him.

To most people, it probably sounds weird that I was basically ready to suit up and show up to walk my father through a graceful and dignified death. However, I've already done it twice before, for other people, and it was the most rewarding thing I have ever done. Plus, this time, I was doing it for one of the people who mattered most to me on earth—my father.

As we were finalizing our plans, CP texted me and told me to meet him at a strip club that our friend Jasper worked at. Our other friend Matt was off the wagon and he wanted my help with what we call a 12th Step. This is where we, as sober people, try to help someone who is not. Our aim is to bring them back into the fold. As soon as I arrived, I enthusiastically burst into the room and screamed my new plan for my parents. CP motioned me to stop. Matt was crying. I took him into my arms. He sobbed harder into them and grabbed me tight. We stayed in this embrace for a solid five minutes. I was honored I was there for my friend, who had just taken me out to dinner two nights prior to soften the sting of being fired.

We spent several hours in the bar. At one point, my phone 'came alive' and started playing Adele's *'Turning Tables.* I noted the irony of the song. Here I was, about to become my toughest critic's guardian—who also happened to be my father. My, the tables had turned! The child who was once told he should only be seen and not heard was about to be the man of the house.

And whilst I did 'make it rain,' at the men's club that day because it seemed fun and ironic, I also got to know a few of the 'entertainers.' Maybe it's weird that I spent hours talking to them about their hopes and dreams, but even in a shady establishment like this, I still am who I am. The dancers liked me. They said they loved my energy and that I had made their day. One even tried to take my shoes. I had more fun there than I probably should have. But soon, we had to go—Matt was only getting drunker and he was now being belligerent and starting fights with other patrons. This was bad for our other friend, Jasper.

CP and I got Matt out of the bar before he got hurt

and we decided to eat at Denny's, where a pure miracle was about to occur.

As we sat and ate, I heard someone call my name. I looked up. "Yes," I responded.

"Aren't you the guy that wrote that book about sobriety?"

"Well, yes," I answered, mock-pushing my hair back, since I don't have any.

"Look, I'm in a lot of trouble and I really need your help," he said.

I could see he was shaking. He explained that he had been in rehab but that he got with a girl right away and that he was now really high and had been for a while. He was also very paranoid and kept telling us there was a hit on him. Matt was still drunk, but CP and I told him we would help him. And we did—a 12th Step within a 12th Step.

We decided that we would take him to a place that is a drop-in shelter for people who are high and in need of a roof over their head before they go into a formal halfway house. I had been here myself on the night of my partner's funeral. As his family had so brutally uninvited me to it, I got so high that I blacked out and walked around barefoot, knocking on doors in a still undisclosed location and asking if I could talk to him.

As we drove to the shelter, our new friend acted more and more paranoid. He asked us several times if we thought there were men with guns in the cars next to us. Then he'd feel ashamed and apologize. I told him that I had used drugs in a Vegas hotel I had been staying at once, and I had thrown pipes away in random trash cans so that I wouldn't get caught. I was also the kind of drug addict who abandoned the very Mariah Carey concert I was there to see in order to rifle through said trash cans and find my long-lost treasure, just so that I could do the only thing I knew how to do back then—get high.

Then I asked him what he was going to do differently this time. He admitted he should probably stay away from girls. Then I said the very words that the paramedic had said to me in that hotel that night: "How can you take care of anyone if you can't take care of yourself?"

I thought about the person in that very hotel hallway. That boy was ruined because his partner was dead and his parents were on their way there. The man sitting in this car wasn't afraid of anything. Unlike that little boy, who was afraid to go to school because boys threw rocks at him, the man in this car knew you could throw boulders at him and he would keep pounding through them until he made sand. I was no longer allowing anything to be thrown at me, I was destroying everything with my superpowers of personal strength and self-love. And I was able to do it because instead of asking random men to fix me, I had been repaired by the Divine Physician himself: God. Yes, the tables really had turned.

We dropped our new friend off to safety. I looked at CP and marveled at how beautiful we were as a team. And because I can be as fearlessly vulnerable as I need to—and can be—with him, I told him how much I loved him and that I was honored to have such an amazing man to move through this sober life with. He responded with the same love and we hugged. Then we did what strong people who fight for others do—we went to a meeting.

During the meeting, I had a stroke of genius. I remembered all the Sundays Pack and I had celebrated a great weekend with a Blizzard from Dairy Queen. I had never shared this hallowed tradition with anyone since he died. So I asked my best friend if he would do me the honor of sharing that experience with me. And like I expected, he was honored to.

Then I sat in the stillness with my best friend as we shared a Blizzard and a beautiful moment together. And I exhaled again.

The Greatest Reward

Being unemployed because of being fired is my greatest fear, and I was about to walk through it to the miracle on the other side.

But first I had to face one of the major tests of my life—one that hurt more than possibly anything I have described thus far. However, it also probably brought me more growth and blessings than I could have ever imagined.

After getting fired from the job where I worked with supposed friends, I applied for unemployment insurance. It's a very small amount of money every week, but given the expense of running my apartment and the sudden reality that my new career had come to a screeching halt, it seemed like a reasonable thing to do in order to protect myself and at least keep a roof over my head.

My former employer did not see it the same way. Though the state had already decided the company had failed to prove I was negligent and there had not been a pattern of wrongdoing on my part, thus making me eligible for the money, my 'friends'—the ones from my men's group who were supposed to support, nurture and encourage me—filed an appeal. There was to be a hearing to determine whether or not I could get—and keep—the unemployment money.

This upped the ante on my fear in a major way. I was in full-on terror mode. I had never been in any kind of trouble in my life, so the idea of a hearing filled me with anxiety. To top it off, the initial hearing was scheduled at the very same time as an incredibly important appointment that we had already scheduled with my mom's very difficult-to-see Alzheimer's doctor. I was able to move the hearing out a week to tend to my mother, but that just gave me more time to hang out in my head, which had become a dangerous neighborhood that I shouldn't have dared to go in alone.

When the day finally came, I braced myself for the worst, and I was right to do so. It was the single most ugly, torturous, horrible, hurtful, demoralizing hour of my sober life. And like every bit of pain from the life that preceded it, I am thankful for it, because it jolted me into a new sense of purpose and a greater love for myself than ever before.

Though they caused me great harm, I will not ever speak badly of these men that I thought were my friends. I will only say they lobbied a series of lies at me that stung deeply. The things they said, all completely untrue, were very hard to hear and sit through. But something very powerful happened: as each lie was levied, I didn't react. I didn't cry. I didn't attack back. I didn't say hurtful things in retaliation. I didn't make up things to make myself sound better. I didn't even say negative things that were true about them or my experience working for them to make them sound worse. When it was my turn to speak, I explained my side of the story honestly, admitting what I had done wrong, apologizing for my part in it, and asking if there was a way I could make things right. I was humble. I was honest. I was kind.

When it was over, I felt like it didn't matter if I won the money or not. I felt like the person who I was in that hearing—a real man of integrity and accountability, who found his power in the art of not reacting to the way other people were treating him—made me a real winner. I even prayed for them to 'win' because I felt if they needed to win so badly, to the point that they would throw me under the bus in the way they had done, they probably needed it more than me. It took two weeks to get the verdict—and it was two full weeks spent in my head, even though my whisper told me my honesty had prevailed.

Not only did I win, but the judge said I was the only witness who came across as credible, which meant more to me than anything. Being seen as who you really are in a stressful, emotional situation like that is something no amount of money can buy.

Another thing happened as a result of that hearing and the hurt I felt from the lies told in it—it woke me up and made me start fighting for myself again. I will admit that being fired as carelessly and callously as I was, led to a pretty major depression. I was also facing a lot of rejection, as although I was applying for similar jobs, places were telling me I didn't have enough experience.

I was nothing like the things these men had said I was though. So I got busy. I had already applied to grad school to get a master's in addiction counseling, but I wasn't willing to be in a situation where anyone could speak the way these men did about me again. So I called Reginald and asked him to detail my car. I thought maybe I could drive people around for a courier service or do something—anything—to get off unemployment. And then, because I moved in the direction of something, the miracles began to rain down on me.

As Reginald was cleaning my car, an old interview I did for my first book on NPR dropped. Then, ten minutes later, I got a call from an agency I'd had an interview with a couple of weeks prior. I was offered a job as a peer support specialist and the best part—the sticking part of the last one—it was during the day. I got to lead groups in various mental health and addiction topics. This is exactly the work I left my corporate job to do and I was finally going to get to do it. On top of that, it was happening because God saw me moving out of my stuckness toward something that was going to better myself.

The fact that I'm going to school as well is the cherry on top. I never would have considered school if I hadn't gotten fired from that job and if I hadn't had a hard time finding a new one afterward. I also did get certified to drive my car for others so I have something to fall back on. I will never again give my power to others in the way I did with those men. That's my part in this—and that is my new power from it.

I also learned another powerful lesson in my interactions with these men I used to look up to: the higher the expectation you put upon others, the greater the fall when they disappoint you or when they fail you. I looked up to these men and expected them to treat me a certain way because we were in a men's group together. Clearly, they did not see me the same way. And that's okay—they are human beings. They are not Gods; therefore they will fail you. Only God is God. Therefore, only He does not fail. I'm grateful for this experience because it strengthened my faith in God and made me realize that He alone is the only man who won't fail me.

I spent my whole life chasing all the wrong ones, begging people to love me. I know that, from now on, I only need to worry about my relationship with God and my relationship with myself. For a person like me, who has been abused since he was five years old, it is nothing short of a miracle to have stepped into this type of personal power.

God is always on time and His plan is always the right one for us. We just have to be patient and willing to work toward it. When we do, we are rewarded with the type of great miracles that can only manifest when we stay close to Him and show up for ourselves in the way I did when I chose not to react to bullying for the first time in my life.

Patrick A. Roland

Like a Prayer

Sometimes not getting what you want can be a wonderful stroke of luck. It probably means God has something even better in store for you.

I know this to be true because of the wild turn of events that landed me back in Las Vegas for the first time since I tried to take my life three years ago.

It started with old behavior almost a year prior. I had been trying to impress Daniel back then and that meant I had to be the chair of the convention for our fellowship. After all, I had been Co-chair the year before and history dictated that I was to ascend to my rightful throne as Chair. The problem with that was, I had real competition. Esther didn't have much more time than I did, sobriety-wise, but she was a very well-known workhorse on committees. She also really wanted to win and made no bones about it. Remember Reece Witherspoon's character in the movie *Election*? She was like that. She won, too. Not by a lot—maybe even only one vote—but my ego didn't like it. I hadn't really delved into prayer and meditation yet, nor had I really changed emotionally—I was still chasing around a twenty-seven-year-old to validate myself, despite the fact he was low-key abusing me. As such, my reaction was less spiritual and more *Mean Girls*. In fact, I'm sure I vowed to destroy her and I'm sure I made a promise not to ever set foot "in her damn convention."

Then a funny thing happened. I was humbled by everything that had happened. I had been broken by experiences which broke me open to a real spiritual experience. It was all because I had been willing to do what Reginald had asked me to do: I got on my knees every day and humbled myself. Sometimes sobbing, sometimes asking, and sometimes begging for God to make me more of who I really was. And so He did.

Now, almost a full year later, I caught wind that the convention was failing. At that particular point, it was in dire straits and things looked bad for it. In fact, they looked bad for our entire fellowship. The moment I heard this news, without any thought or pretense, I did something I never thought I would ever do: I reached across the aisle and asked Esther, my 'enemy', if she needed help. And the next thing I knew, I was working hand-in-hand with the very person I said I would never forgive. How could I? She took my rightful chair from me! But she gave me so much more than a leadership position. She gave me the opportunity to step up and show real leadership. I guess deep down I'm not sour, stung, hurt and unforgiving. Who I really am is a person who offers grace, gratitude and love to a person who, in her quest for power, stepped all over mine.

So I ended up playing a major role in social media management on the very committee I had selfishly boycotted. Now, because of my selflessness, a miracle was about to be given to me.

I had called the sponsor hotel to get a room for the weekend of the convention, but I decided the expense was too high. While I was on the phone with the hotel, they asked me if I would hold the line to listen to a special offer. I have no idea why I stayed on the line—it must have been an act of God—but before I knew it, I was being talked into a menagerie of really exciting vacation destinations. The lady first started talking about California, but then very randomly—or perhaps not so—she became almost insistent that I seemed like the type of guy who liked Las Vegas.

I was like, "Oh honey, if only you knew." But the more she kept talking, the more I kept thinking that perhaps I needed to make peace with the city where I had both lost and found myself. I knew Mariah had just inked a deal to go back. When the woman offered me a deal to go to Vegas for three nights for $99, I couldn't say no. So I said yes. I had no idea I was about to create magic.

About two days later, CP told me that his family was moving to Las Vegas, and he really wanted to go see them sometime. He was still with Melissa though, so I figured he would take her. I focused on going to see Mariah.

Then, almost out of nowhere, CP and Melissa broke up for a short time. He called me almost immediately and said: "Make that reservation. We're going to Vegas."

I was elated. Not just about the trip, but also because I was the guy who hadn't been allowed to meet his partner's family and was then kicked out of his own house and disinvited to his dead lover's funeral. There was something about being worthy of meeting my best friend's family that made me feel particularly loved. It was a full circle moment—God was giving me something back that had been taken from me. It was my reward for being patient and loving to people who hadn't always treated me that way.

CP invited another friend, AA, and the three of us set off for what I can honestly say was the best vacation of my life. I got on my knees and prayed before we left—you never know what a trip like that is going to be like, especially as we were three very different people—but once we got on our way, I felt my prayers being answered. I felt the power of God that whole weekend. I even felt the presence of Pack, and felt that song he played at the end of his life—*Safe and Sound*—playing out in real time as I reclaimed Las Vegas with my best friends.

As the weekend played out, each of us took turns doing what we wanted. Most of my goals involved buying sparkly shoes at the shop where I bought my very first pair. Most of theirs involved gambling. It shouldn't be surprising that as I was buying two new pairs of sparkly marvels, CP won $400 in the slot machine across the way. I personally believe that speaks to the magic of the shoes and the miracles they will continue to manifest as long as I keep passionately charging ahead in them.

Then we met his family. I always wondered how this super jock and I—a super flaming queen—became best friends. However, I figured it out almost instantly when I realized his cousin was a married lesbian who, just like me, took care of her parents. She—just like me—also worried about them as they aged and had similar medical issues.

These wonderful people—these giving, loving, breathing, functional, fun, funny, happy, joyful, beautiful people—made me feel welcome and loved instantly. They seemed so close, and there was so much love between them. I knew CP better by meeting these people.

It wasn't just a cursory dinner where you exchange pleasantries. Unlike the man I was basically married to, who was ashamed of himself and therefore ashamed of me, CP proved he was proud of me. He asked me to tell them my story. So I told them all of it and they showed me love and compassion with kindness in their eyes. They hugged me and held on tight to make sure I felt it. They told me I was amazing and that they were proud of me. They told me they loved me and that I was in their family now; that I was always welcome there. They saw and heard me, accepting me exactly as I was. Not only was I "good enough," I was enough, because that's who I showed them I was.

In just a few hours in the very city where I almost gave everything of me away, these people gave everything back to me. These loving, kind people did want me and it made me realize the most important thing I think I will ever realize: I'll never again long for the ones I didn't get because God gave me the ones I was supposed to have. It was like He was doing surgery on my broken heart and CP was the doctor. I know that I am responsible for my own happiness and I know I fixed myself, but I'm always going give CP a little credit for breathing life into the parts of me that even I had given up on. That's the kind of friendship—a real deep, from the heart kind of love—that you know is always going to persevere. And that kind of friendship can only come from God.

Somehow, the trip got even better after my open-heart surgery. I had jokingly mentioned that I wanted to go see Magic Mike Live. I expected both of my super masculine, heterosexual friends to tell me to take a flying leap. But while CP bristled a little at the thought, both were open to it. AA was even encouraging. I felt a greater force working in this too. When Pack was alive, he was so uncomfortable with his sexuality that he wouldn't see Magic Mike with me in the theatre. Obviously, we fought about it; but ultimately, I went by myself. I felt like *something* was helping me get to that show. Maybe it was my repentant dead lover who was trying to make things right from wherever he was now.

I used to think I was only going to be abused by men because that's all I knew. But the truth is, that's what I allowed. Now I do not. I stand up for myself, I love myself and I show others the real Patrick Roland. Because of that, I got to see Magic Mike Live with my two brothers. They loved and accepted me exactly as I was and all they wanted was for me to be happy, so they were willing to do this with me.

That's what friendship is. That's what brotherhood is. THAT is what love is. And I am in awe that I got to survive and get sober to experience this kind of life. It was nothing short of a miracle. I couldn't believe I had gone from trying to jump out of a window to end my life the last time I was there to this. I guess sobriety really does suit me. We took pictures at the show and in them, I am smiling brighter, bigger and more joyfully than I have ever done before.

The next day, as we were driving home to Phoenix, I was trying to be polite and play rap music. AA suggested I play what I wanted.

"You're aware that's going to be a super gay mix of Whitney Houston, Madonna and Bette Midler?" I asked.

"I'd expect nothing less," he said.

The Sparkle King

I must add, AA is even more ripped than CP—they met in jail—and I doubt he's ever been friends with anyone like me. I wouldn't know it though. I feel like the three of us are real brothers, like we were always supposed to find each other and become friends. We belong together.

On the way home, we all jammed out to my super gay music and both CP and AA danced and sang along. There happens to be more Celine Dion in my mix than I remembered, but the Titanic song for never played. So AA began chanting: "I want the *Titanic* song. I want the *Titanic* song." It never did play, though I enjoyed his effort to step up and 'queen out' for me.

Later, CP really wanted to hear *'Like a Prayer'* by Madonna. But even though I have, like, nine versions of it, it took about fifteen minutes and a near crash to find it. Soon, however, we were all jamming to Madonna. Two hyper-masculine former felons and a flaming gay guy were all now connected by something much bigger than anything else in the world: love.

Later that day, when I was at home, I was listening to music. I know that the second song I hear is always from Pack so I paid close attention to it. On this occasion, it was *'The Sign'* by Ace of Base.

"Okay Pack. Tell me. What's the sign?" I asked out loud.

The next thing I knew, the Titanic song was playing. Tears streamed down my cheeks. I felt the power of God's presence and a knowing from within that we had not been alone that day. Something I had already suspected.

I got on my knees and prayed. As I did, I sobbed. I thanked God for giving me what I had always wanted: friends that were really brothers. As I prayed for CP and AA, my Chihuahua Chloe stepped on my phone. I started to curse her out, but soon I was crying harder. Somehow, she had made the phone come alive and it was playing 'Like a Prayer.'

Knowing all my prayers had been heard and that we

had been protected and guided in Vegas, I thanked God even more and continued to pray for my brothers while our song played out loud. Because life may very well be a mystery, but I know for sure what is not. If it feels this much like love, it can't be anything other than God.

The Sparkle King

Patrick A. Roland

Through it All

When I was unemployed and being beaten by a man who didn't love me, I had such low self-esteem that I set out on a self-destructive course to destroy my life with drugs. After I left my corporate job and failed at my first attempt in the behavioral health field, I used all of my free time to get closer to God through prayer and meditation. I consider every moment a blessing. The gratitude I have for much of it overwhelms me.

I got to go to lunch with my parents on their 48th anniversary. They held hands when they walked into the restaurant. It might have been the most beautiful thing I've ever seen. I was grateful for that moment because just a few days later, my mother moved out of their condo. She's getting full-time care now and I feel particularly proud of this because I was present for every doctor's appointment. I held her hand when she received her official Alzheimer's diagnosis. I put my life on hold to make sure the rest of hers was safe and taken care of. I had to. It was my duty. She saved my life when she called the cops on me in Vegas. How could I not drop everything to make sure I took care of hers? She's doing well—she's reading books. She has a new doctor. She smiles more and looks like herself again. She is still obviously confused and definitely dealing with memory issues, but she is safe and happy. I almost jumped out of a window because I was afraid of facing that duty but I did, and I'm here to say that if I do nothing else in this life, at least I did what I could to give her the best life she can have.

The transition of moving to my dad's hasn't been easy. I had been questioning my decision to do so because I had felt a palpable disinterest—maybe even anger—coming from him. He had only said about four sentences to me for the first several weeks I had spent there with him. It may also have been grief. I can't imagine it's easy to lose your partner of forty-eight years. It was hard to lose my partner of three.

Still, I knew he struggled with the groceries because of his Parkinson's, so I offered to help him at the grocery store one recent Saturday.

When we got to the store, the magic happened. The man who I thought didn't pay any attention to me seemed to know everything about me.

It started with a box of Honey Nut Cheerios.

Every aisle we went down, he pointed to something I had eaten in the last two weeks and asked me if I wanted more of it.

It was as if forty-three years of difficulty and awkwardness disappeared and for the first time, a father and a son became real friends. I felt like my father saw me for the first time in my life that day, and that made me feel more love than I could ever imagine.

The next day was Father's Day. Usually I write something generic, unfeeling or boring because that is what I have always thought he wanted. But one thing I keep learning in sobriety is that the more authentic and real we are with people, the more we move toward the relationship we really want with them.

So Instead of two lines of fluff, I told my dad the truth. I shared real feelings with him.

After he read the card, something happened that had never happened before: my father, quiet and stoic, started talking to me. And he kept talking. And before I knew it, we were engulfed in probably the longest and most meaningful conversation of our lives.

Because I was willing to be vulnerable and show him who I really was.

We don't always have an easy relationship but the blessing here is that we do have *a* relationship. We never had one before, so if we can get this far in about a month, imagine the possibilities for the future as I continue to pray for our relationship to grow.

I've quickly realized that I always expected him to be my hero and I was always disappointed because he couldn't be. But when I stepped up and became his hero–because that is closer to the truth of who I really am–I stopped feeling disappointed by broken expectations and started feeling the love and respect I always deserved from him.

Recently we were driving home from visiting my mother. Seeing her makes him anxious and he was particularly so on this day. I asked him why he didn't just move back to Iowa and get care there.

"You'd be happier there," I said.

"I could never leave your mother," he replied.

"I don't think you need to worry about her anymore," I said. "I've got this."

His response to this moved me and forced me to see that the story I kept telling that we had a difficult relationship that couldn't be repaired was just that, a story. And it was no longer true:

"The truth is, I don't ever want to be away from you again," he said.

I get a lot of respect and love for the way I treat my parents but it all goes back to what that paramedic said to me in that hotel in Vegas. I couldn't take care of them until I could take care of myself. And because I do such a good job of showing up for myself today, I have finally been able to show up for them in the way I always wanted to. I'd rather be the guy that gets up on the ladder and fixes the smoke alarm or air filter than the one who shows up high at his father's 75th birthday party. The former is who I really am, and that's who they see today.

And because I am that person at home, I get to show up for myself in the world today as that guy as well. The very week I was going through that awful hearing, I was asked to speak in front of a large group of people I didn't know. I worked the pain of that experience into my story. I was real. I was broken. I was human. I was honest. I was vulnerable. I put myself back together in front of these people and in all of that raw energy, I spoke with a passion and fire that felt like something not of me. It was God making me more of what I really am—what I pray for.

When I was done, these strangers—friends now—filled my heart with the love that had been taken from me earlier in the week by haters.

"You're the best speaker I've ever heard," one lady said.

"You were so honest, I could feel your heart beating from all the way up there to here," said another.

"I had a lot of sober time here before I relapsed but I'm new again. I was afraid to come back," said a man at the back, who had relapsed and just come back to the rooms. "But I want you to know that I have less than twenty-four hours and just yesterday, I felt dead. You breathed life in to me again."

And then, when it was over, a woman stood before me. She trembled in fear and tears streamed down her face. She told me it was only her second meeting ever.

"You told MY story tonight," she said. "And because of you, I know I belong here and I am going to keep coming back."

There's no greater feeling than being seen as who you really are. When people that are just like you take the time to tell you that you made a difference in their life by sharing your truth, you'd better appreciate it, because that is God's voice reminding you that you are on the right track. You are doing the next right thing.

Helping someone else is always the right thing to do. Even if you feel like you have nothing, the act of giving creates more abundance. Also, the truth is, if someone asks you then it probably means you have more. That does not mean you let people walk all over you—boundaries are important—but I do know that giving creates receiving. So if you desire God's gifts, keep giving yours and you will receive the benefits of all His glory.

I just want you to know that if you're broken and you have lost hope, don't give up. I can tell you from experience that it's always darkest before it gets the brightest. And no matter what you are experiencing, things *can* and *will* get so bright that the light will blind you.

All you have to do is have a little faith, love yourself, and believe you can. Keep repeating that and you can make just about anything you want come true. And you can trust me—I was there. I get it. You think you're done, but you're not. You have so much potential. You're gonna make it. You are beautiful and if I can do it, I know you can.

So I hope this reaches someone: I have faith in you, I love you and I believe you can do it. You are enough. I know this, because I am too.

Just a few years ago, I was ready to give everything up and jump out of that window. But I didn't. I stayed. I loved. I learned. I sparkled. I hurt. I cried. I clung to people. I lost people. I lost things. I cried more. I dug in to service work. I found God. I began to pray. I began to meditate. I cried more. I began to pray more.

I'm not here to say it's always easy because life is anything but that. But it's worth it. You're worth it. You're beautiful. God created you for a very specific reason and He loves you very much. If an overweight gay, bipolar, alcoholic, addict who's a widowed abuse survivor can bear witness to the majestic glory and power of God, then anyone can. I was told He didn't love me because of who I was and I know that is a lie because I can feel him working through me as I write these words right now.

So if you feel like you are done, you don't have to be. Follow your sparkle and live out your dream. If I can do it, anyone can. I'm days away from starting a new job in the field I chose—at middle age, I want to add. I also just started grad school, I have two elderly parents who require attention and care, I just released a second children's book and I have multiple commitments in the

12-step program that keeps me sober. I fought hard for the life I always wanted because I know I deserve it. I also know God does too.

As I drove away from my first day of grad school, the Whitney Houston version of *'Higher Love'* began playing. It was this very song that I used to listen to when I closed my eyes and prayed for a higher love, one that would provide the kind of magic and miracles I had always dreamed of. I drove in the direction of my new life—the one full of blessings, friendship and love that I had created by following my whisper, which directed me out of situations that no longer served me. And I felt happier than I ever had, because I loved myself and trusted God enough to do so too.

Patrick A. Roland

The Heart of the Matter

A spiritual person chooses happiness over and over and over again and by doing so, they live in the ecstasy of God. I plan to sparkle as bright as I possibly can so that my gift—my light—continues to bring me closer to the God I serve, and closer yet to the man I know I really am.

I choose to be grateful for all the pain in my past so that I can continue to generate power from it. I know that gratitude opens up a space full of light in my soul for grace to seep into. If I stay in this beautiful space of acceptance and the Divine, I actually can become grace. That means I get to grow into my true self—my higher self—and openly and knowingly trudge the happy road of destiny laid before me by God. And because I serve a loving, patient God, I know for sure that if I can do it, so can you.

You can either be happy or you can be right. After spending years in misery and depression—and then in the abyss of the dangerous intersection of grief and addiction—I choose to be happy. I'd rather just accept that I can't do anything about how Daniel or anyone else feels about me. I pray for him and forgive him for the way he treated me. It doesn't mean he didn't hurt me or that it didn't happen, it just means that I am strong enough to let myself heal and move on from it. It means I won't let his actions consume me. It means I can let him stay broken. It means he can be petty and not speak to me because I know his behavior says more about him than it does me. It means that I can get close to someone else like CP, who actually wants to love me, because he is capable of it. Because of this, I actually see the broken way Daniel treated me as a blessing. In a way, he set me free so that I could receive the love I deserve. It's kind of my own *'I Will Always Love You'* moment. I finally get to be Whitney!

The cherry on the cake of my life is that I actually found God in it. I know many people don't ever get to revel in His eternal love and glory. For this gift alone, I know how blessed I am. The desperate loneliness I once felt that almost derailed my sparkle completely has now been fulfilled by the promise of love that only a relationship with God can provide. That doesn't mean I don't get sad or even still live with bipolar depression; it just means I humbly get on my knees and ask for help when I do. And God always shows up when I ask him to.

You can make a big positive difference in the world with each positive thought you hold. Multiply those positive thoughts by sharing them with others so that love and light can manifest the miracle of joy. Watch as your world shifts in this positive space—you'll see the gifts of grace, gratitude, love, light and forgiveness come to life in your midst. Set yourself free from ties that bind you and let yourself feel the joy that comes from acceptance. Let yourself handle situations that would have ended you before you discovered your power.

Everything that happened last fall—the dishonest publicist, Daniel, the job discomfort, the suddenly abusive boyfriend—happened to me in the past. All of them gave me the opportunity to make decisions that honored myself. I got to let myself grow, instead of shrinking back into old habits and behaviors. I got to show up for myself, and in turn, show myself who I really am. I guess I better be grateful for myself then, too.

I am an overweight middle-aged gay man who lives with bipolar. I am an alcoholic and a drug addict. I have been a widow since I found my partner dead in our home. I became homeless and unable to properly grieve because of homophobia. I have been abused by men I thought loved me. I have been bullied by others since I was in Kindergarten. And you know what? I choose forgiveness for all of it. I forgive myself for letting all of that happen to myself—because the truth is, I was the common denominator in all of it. I forgive every individual who was part of the painful puzzle I have now put together as the power that is me. The man I am today is whole, alive, safe, and in love with everything about this beautiful and sometimes busted life we live as human beings. I can say "I love you more than this argument" and end months of bitterness and arguing. I can also accept that I may say that to someone and still be denied by them. And that's fine—they are allowed to have their experience. You be you, boo—Just let me be me. Let me like me. Let me love me. Let me choose me. In this space of forgiveness and gratitude, I have opened the door for grace to take over and let my sparkle burn. It is in this light—which is really a spiritually-blessed fire from deep within the pit of my soul—that I show others my beauty. They get to see who I really am and what I am capable of. And if you can't figure it out, let me break it down: I CAN do anything I choose to do. All I have to do is love myself and believe I can. And because I've never loved myself more, it's a guaranteed win. All of the above applies to you too—stop listening to the voices inside your head that say you can't do something and start following the one inside your heart that knows you can. Just like me, you are enough too!

My earliest memory is that of other boys throwing rocks at me whilst I waited for the bus. However, because I have shown people who I really am by living my truth and being myself, my life is a lot different now. Recently, the beautiful, light-shifiing shoes that became my staple started giving me blisters. I was in so much pain, I could barely walk. I spent a whole weekend at a convention limping around Denver with Reginald and CP. I never complained, but Reginald set into motion an afternoon that made me believe I really was a king.

Reginald suggested I needed bigger shoes—perhaps tennis shoes—to alleviate my pain. I bristled at the idea of losing my trademark shoes. I was also open to it because I know that when I follow Reginald's advice, I always end up living my best life. So I told him I would look at new shoes with one caveat: they had to sparkle. So we spent about an hour in a department store, where my sponsor kept picking out shoes for me to wear. I struggled with that because of the pain my feet were in, so CP lovingly stepped forward and carefully slid several pairs of shoes on and off my feet until we found the right pair—tennis shoes that sparkled.

As I was standing in line to buy the shoes, I began to cry.

"Why are you crying," CP asked.

"Because all I have ever known from men is cruelty and abuse and I never believed two men would love me enough to help me in the way you two did today," I said.

"Well we do," CP responded. "And I promise you that's never going to change."

I know I received this love because I showed these men the man I really am. And in their reflection, I see the real me: a man who never again has to put up with someone else's bullshit because I choose myself over and over again. Because when you stand up for yourself with the type of magical self-love I do, the miracle that is love shows up for you, over and over again. You just have to do as I do, and demand it by being unapologetically you.

And so it is. When I am grateful I find my grace. When I live in forgiveness, I allow my heart to heal so that I can move forward. When I choose to love myself, I allow myself to grow and do things I never imagined. And when I bask in the blinding, beautiful and radiant light that is my sparkle, I dance mightily and excitedly along the journey to the joy that I've found in long-term sobriety. It is in this light that I move closer to who I really am; it is in this light where I become one with God and we reveal our greatest mutual creation yet: *The Sparkle King.*

Epilogue - Life is Beautiful

Of all the things I have written about that I have conquered, I still do experience the lows that occur as a result of living with bipolar depression. It's a part of me and a part of my body's chemistry that has been there all of my forty-three years. I share my experiences for people like me, who are looking to find their own sparkle.

I know these feelings will go away because I can point to a lifetime of experiences where they always do. So instead of fighting it, I lean into the pain so that it can become tomorrow's power. I'm not afraid of going into dark places—just for a visit—because I know how powerful the light is after these experiences pass.

This isn't a whole lot different from faith. I was walking the dogs recently and I couldn't find any feathers. I'm very good at spotting and cherishing them. They are a sign that God and my favorite angel Pack are guiding me on my journey to joy. As a result, they give me hope. I stopped and prayed: "God, I'm having a hard time; can you please show me a feather to show me there IS hope?"

And then, just like that, I found one. And then another and another. Then several more. Before I knew it, all I saw was feathers. Because no matter what you are experiencing, there is always hope.

Hold the intention of seeing all the beauty in life and that is what you will see. Take a look in the mirror and rejoice in the remarkable, joyous, wonderful, amazing visage that is you. If you only knew how many miracles it took for you to be standing there, you would dance and feel true gratitude. You would realize that you belong in the infinite dance that is life. It is my deepest desire that you do realize this. Because no one else is you and that is your power.

Life is beautiful. It can hurt, it can be strange, it can be awful, it can be hard, it can be dark, and it can be scary—but I promise you, there is always a light at the end of the tunnel. It's never over until it is. And if there isn't light yet, that is a sign it is not over.

Because if someone is gonna make it, that someone oughta be you. The most beautiful man I ever knew said that to me and even though things got harder and darker, they eventually got brighter and more beautiful. All I had to do was step into my sparkle and look closer. Life is a series of miracles. We have the power from within to make changes in our lives and to experience joy and fulfillment. It's in that power—generated from our positive attitude—that we get to shift the quality of our lives and love ourselves as we deserve.

You are the light of the world. Do not hide your light. Let whatever song you sing shine its way into life with a joyful noise. This song is the music of your life! Cultivate it. Raise your vibration and let God work through you, and with you, to let your light shine! Because that is where you sparkle, too.

I have come a long way from the man who didn't think he deserved the initial success and acclaim he received that fateful New Year's Eve when I became The Sparkle King. Now, when people ask me how I am, I smile with my eyes and I speak joyfully and truthfully from the heart: I have my sparkle back and I'm going to fight to keep it. Because I *do* deserve it.

Patrick A. Roland

THE BEGINNING

The Sparkle King

Patrick A. Roland

About the Author

Patrick A. Roland is a gay, bipolar, ex-drug addict, widowed abuse survivor and the author of three great books. His first, *Unpacked Sparkle: a Story of Grief and Recovery*, kicks off his journey of sobriety and self-love following the death of his partner, Pack, in January 2014. This book was published by Az Publishing and is available on Amazon.

His second book is a children's book called *Sparkle On!* This book is about a gecko who is constantly constant bullied but chooses to fight this with love.

His new book, *The Sparkle King*, keeps the sparkle flowing as Patrick finds his way through several fear-inducing experiences by constantly choosing faith to overcome them in long-term sobriety.

Patrick lives in Phoenix, Arizona. He is a peer support at a mental health clinic, where he helps others just like himself. He's also earning a Master's in Addiction Counselling at Grand Canyon University and is taking care of his elderly, terminally ill parents. He wants you to know you can do anything you decide to do if you love yourself.

www.ingramcontent.com/pod-product-compliance
Lightning Source LLC
Chambersburg PA
CBHW070103080526
44586CB00013B/1167